the GOD who won't Let go

Other Recent Books by Dean Merrill

Sinners in the Hands of an Angry Church
Fresh Wind, Fresh Fire, with Jim Cymbala
Together at Home, with Grace Merrill
Wait Quietly

GETTING A SECOND CHANCE FROM

the GOD WHO
won't Let go

DIVINE grace in the face of guilt,
tragedy, and failure

FORMERLY TITLED *ANOTHER CHANCE*

Dean Merrill

ZondervanPublishingHouse
Grand Rapids, Michigan

A Division of HarperCollinsPublishers

The God Who Won't Let Go
Copyright © 1981, 1998 by Dean Merrill

Revised edition of *Another Chance: How God Overrides Our Big Mistakes*

Requests for information should be addressed to:

📖 ZondervanPublishingHouse
Grand Rapids, Michigan 49530

Library of Congress Cataloging-in-Publication Data

Merrill, Dean.
    The God who won't let go : divine grace in the face of guilt, tragedy, and failure / Dean Merrill.
        p.   cm.
    Includes bibliographical references.
    ISBN 0-310-21848-9 (softcover)
    1. Suffering—Religious aspects—Christianity. 2. Guilt—Religious aspects—Christianity. 3. Failure (Christian theology). 4. Grace (Theology). 5. Consolation. I. Title.
BV4909.M47   1998
248.8'6—dc21   97-41433
                                                                                                        CIP

Pages 55–60 reprinted from *Where Eagles Soar* © 1980 by Jamie Buckingham. Published by Chosen Books Publishing Co., Ltd., Lincoln, VA 22078. Used by permission.

Pages 105–108 excerpted from *Let Us Enjoy Forgiveness* by Judson Cornwall © 1978 by Judson Cornwall. Published by Fleming H. Revell Company. Used by permission.

Pages 111–112 reprinted with permission from "Waiting" © 1978 by Christian Medical Society.

Interior design by Dan Hyma and Sue Vandenberg Koppenol

Printed in the United States of America

---

98 99 00 01 02 03 04 /❖ DC/ 10 9 8 7 6 5 4 3 2 1

With gratitude . . .

To each of the courageous people who shared their life experience with me for inclusion in this book.

To John Sprecher, Charles Nestor, Daryl Merrill, and others who introduced me to those courageous people.

To Leighton Ford, Richard Dobbins, John Freeman, Bob Brenneman, and many others whose insights into the process of restoration stretched my understanding.

To Bob and Marilyn Pollitt, who provided the quiet room where this manuscript was born.

To Grace, my wife, who taught me to care for those who hurt.

contents

PART FOUR
MOVING ON

Restoration

The sheep goes now
Toward the distant slope
Where taller, tastier grass awaits.
Let the ninety and nine stay bleating and bumping one another—
The horizon calls.

He's one of your flock, Good Shepherd,
And he's heading for the ravine.
He doesn't understand drop-offs
And wolves
And how soon darkness will fall upon the land.
Call him back! Stop him!

The meadow shrinks in the gathering dusk
And the Shepherd's ram,
Full but unsatisfied,
Edges toward the rim
Until in a clatter of gravel and dust
He plummets into the gorge
Brambles clawing at his wool—
He lies stunned upon his back.

He cannot rise; he cannot reverse
The steps that brought him to this dreadful place;
He can, in fact, do nothing at all.
A cold moon stares down at him
While sounds of night intensify;
He is trapped—but more
He is alone.

A flickering lamp, footsteps in the underbrush,
The chill and darkness are foiled this time
As muscled arms encircle the fallen one
And hoist him from the stones and mud
To ride upon tall shoulders
Back to the village fold.

Had you nothing else to do this night, Good Shepherd?
Should not this rebel sheep of yours be ousted
From care and food and drink for this?
He chose his independent path—
Will he yet be welcome in your flock?

The Shepherd answers not; he is too busy
Calling friends and neighbors,
The young and old about the town,
And even angels hear his shout:
"Rejoice with me! I have found
My sheep that was lost!
He was mine before; he is mine tonight;
He shall be mine forever!
Rejoice, rejoice."

The villagers cheer,
And light-years distant,
The cherubim slap each other
On the back—
Both earth and heaven are awake tonight
For the jubilee that crowns
The restoration of a single sheep.

the Return
of confidence

the god of
the second chance

I believe in the God of the second chance.

I believe in the God who is not put off by our fiascoes.

I believe in the God who has an uncanny ability to bring good out of disaster.

I believe in the God who puts Humpty Dumpties back together again.

He is the God, in fact, whose "mercy endureth forever." How many times have we recited those words without absorbing their meaning. His mercy has no cutoff. It goes on . . . and on . . . and on. . . .

It endures for the person who has made an undeniable mistake in his life, whose future has been torpedoed by one or more fateful acts. The person who has stepped outside of his marriage . . . the trusted employee who has mishandled corporate funds . . . the woman who has borne an illegitimate child . . . the young man who has rejected his early faith and turned instead to drugs or alcohol . . . the person who has betrayed his family, his friends. . . .

Divine mercy reaches as well to the person who has not committed an overt act of wrong, but has rather made a bad decision. It made sense enough at the time of choosing, but with hindsight, it turns out to have been tragic. The person who left a job when he should have stayed . . . or stayed when he should have left . . . or quit school too soon, thereby limiting future advancement . . . or got into hopeless debt . . . or sent his child to the wrong school, triggering a barrage of negative effects . . . or started a business that flopped.

Does God hold on to such children? When their dreams have been smashed, when self-confidence has fled, when the future goes blank, when even fellow Christians shake their heads and look the other way—is the Father's patience exhausted, too? Let him speak for himself:

> *"I will restore you to health*
> *and heal your wounds,"*
>   *declares the LORD,*
> *"because you are called an outcast,*
>   *Zion for whom no one cares."*
>
> Jeremiah 30:17

> *I live in a high and holy place,*
>   *but also with him who is contrite and lowly in spirit,*
> *to revive the spirit of the lowly*
>   *and to revive the heart of the contrite.*
> *I will not accuse forever,*
>   *nor will I always be angry,*
> *for then the spirit of man would grow faint before me—*
>   *the breath of man that I have created. . . .*
> *I have seen his ways, but I will heal him;*
>   *I will guide him and restore comfort to him.*
>
> Isaiah 57:15–16, 18

David, who made more than one spectacular error and was still hailed in the New Testament as a man who "served God's purpose in his own generation" (Acts 13:36), gives us some touching glimpses of the God he knew:

> *I will exalt you, O LORD,*
> *   for you lifted me out of the depths. . . .*
> *Your turned my wailing into dancing;*
> *   you removed my sackcloth and clothed me with joy,*
> *that my heart may sing to you and not be silent.*
> *O LORD my God, I will give you thanks forever.*
>
> Psalm 30:1, 11–12

It is at this point—"Who is God, and what kind of God is he?"—that we must begin. We must return to our Source, our Refuge. What he thinks of us, now that we have blown it, will have a greater impact on our future than almost anything else.

We may fear to approach him; in fact, he may be the *last* person we want to confront, schooled as we are in teachings about his blazing holiness, his disgust for sin, his absolute purity.

But on the other hand, he has been watching over a planet of imperfect children for a very long time. What we have done was hardly a shock to him. He has seen it many times before. Furthermore, he is the only one who has both the power and the will to redeem the situation.

The advice of our times can mislead us. We are told, in various ways, "To move back to former things is regression. Faith is an element of childhood. Belief is something you cling to in your early crises, until you come to a more mature way of coping."

The good news to adults who have made a major mistake in their lives is this: *It's okay to run to your Father.* In fact, it's the smartest thing you can do at the moment. It is your one route to freedom from the confusion, guilt, shame, and self-doubt that

hammer at your sanity. In the words of Paul Johnson's con-
temporary Christian song:

> *He didn't bring us this far to leave us;*
> *He didn't teach us to swim to let us drown.*
> *He didn't build his home in us to move away;*
> *He didn't lift us up to let us down.*

In the ancient world, a well-known legend told about a
rather marvelous bird called the phoenix, which lived in splen-
dor in the Far East. Its home was a grove of trees untouched by
violence, fear, or grief of any kind, perpetually green and ver-
dant. The phoenix passed its time with singing and reveling
in utopian joys on all sides.

But once every five hundred years, it left its home for the
world of death. It flew to Syria, built a nest in the top of a palm
tree, and set fire to itself. Amazingly, from its ashes a worm
emerged, which developed a cocoon and soon became a new,
young phoenix bird ready to return to the East and begin the
life-cycle again.

A farfetched myth—except that more than a few early
Christians saw within it an illustration of a central theme of the
Gospel: resurrection. Clement of Rome retold the story in his
First Letter (chapters 25–26) as he was making the point that
God brings life out of death, not only in the case of his Son,
but in us as well. We are the receivers of something inextin-
guishable: eternal life, a force meant to show itself in the present as well as the future. In the midst of a world that is dying,
we can rise from our own ashes. We can live again.

Says Paul: "We have this treasure in jars of clay to show
that this all-surpassing power is from God and not from us. We
are hard pressed on every side, but not crushed; perplexed,
but not in despair; persecuted, but not abandoned; struck down,
but not destroyed. We always carry around in our body the
death of Jesus, so that the life of Jesus may also be revealed in

our body. For we who are alive are always being given over to death for Jesus' sake, so that his life may be revealed in our mortal body. . . .

"Therefore we do not lose heart. Though outwardly we are wasting away, yet inwardly we are being renewed day by day. . . . So *we fix our eyes* not on what is seen, but *on what is unseen*. For what is seen is temporary, but what is unseen is eternal" (2 Cor. 4:7–11, 16, 18, italics added).

And that is what the rest of this book is about. It will show you some of the means God uses to bring life out of death, renewed potential out of disappointment and downfall. It will introduce you to people who have been through a self-inflicted ordeal and have come through to sunshine once again. They are not perfect people; they have not necessarily done everything right since their fall. They are rather a cross-section to show that restoration *can* happen. Their stories and the other parts of this book will help you answer the question "Where do I go from here?"

The Holy Spirit, after all, is called the Counselor four different times in Scripture. Long before modern psychotherapy began trying to help persons in stress, the Spirit was restoring and renewing, guiding men and women through the white water rapids of their lives to the quiet pools beyond. He is the same today.

For Your Reflection

1. What was your view of God as a child? Was he most like a judge? A grandfather? A school principal? What?
2. Now that you're older, how do you view him? Has he become friendlier over the years? More stern? Or about the same?

3. What did you read in this chapter that made you say, "Yes, but—"? Were your objections valid?
4. If you really believed that God gave second chances in this life, what differences would it make in your feelings about yourself?

what now?

If I found I had driven into a bog, I should know I had missed the road. But this knowledge would not be of much comfort if I then had to stand helpless watching the car sink and vanish: the damage would be done, and that would be that. Is it the same when a Christian wakes up to the fact that he has missed God's guidance and taken the wrong way? Is the damage irrevocable? Must he now be put off course for life? Thank God, no. Our God is a God who not merely restores, but takes up our mistakes and follies into His plan for us and brings good out of them. This is part of the wonder of His gracious sovereignty. "I will restore to you the years that the locust has eaten. . . ." God makes not only the wrath of man to turn to His praise but the misadventures of Christians too.

—J. I. Packer
Knowing God, pp. 219–20

a LIttLe

tHING CaLLeD HOPe

He began with all the right connections. His mother was a prominent woman in the Jerusalem church, their spacious home a meeting place for part of the huge congregation. The apostle Peter had come to their door first upon his miraculous release from prison (Acts 12) to break the news that prayer had been answered.

His cousin was the gentle, respected Barnabas, donor of real-estate funds to the work of the church, "a good man, full of the Holy Spirit and faith" (Acts 11:24). Thus it was not a total surprise that when Barnabas and Paul were set apart by the Antioch believers for the first missionary journey, a historic new venture into the Mediterranean world, "John was with them as their helper" (Acts 13:5). His future was bright.

But sometime in the next few weeks, all that changed. The Scriptures do not tell us why or how. Perhaps the crossing of the open water to Cyprus was frightening; perhaps the tension of the appearance before the proconsul, when Paul suddenly called for a sorcerer to be struck blind, took its toll. Perhaps the young man was irritated at the secondary role that was falling to his relative as Paul's ministry flourished. Whatever the cause, John Mark stuck it out for one more voyage, to Perga on the mainland, and then made the mistake of his life. He "left them to return to Jerusalem" (Acts 13:13).

What he said upon his arrival we do not know. But we do know that he had seared his worthlessness into the memory of Paul. Two years later, when Paul and Barnabas began planning their second extended trip abroad, the name of John Mark was raised. "Absolutely not," declared the apostle. "He deserted us last time. He's useless."

Barnabas could not agree, and invited his cousin to go along on a separate mission to Cyprus. But we cannot help noticing in Acts 15:40 that it was Paul and his new associate, Silas, who left "commended by the brothers to the grace of the Lord." Their exploits take up the next two and one-half chapters of the Bible, while not a further word is said about Barnabas and John Mark's trip.

Was his career forever doomed? Could God do anything with a quitter? Would the church ever give him another opportunity?

Fifteen years pass before the answer comes, in the writings of Paul from a Roman prison. His traveling days are now finished; he must rely upon his pen and his colleagues in the ministry:

"My fellow prisoner Aristarchus sends you his greetings, as does Mark, the cousin of Barnabas. (You have received instructions about him; if he comes to you, welcome him)" (Col. 4:10).

"Epaphras ... sends you greetings. And so do Mark, Aristarchus, Demas and Luke, my fellow workers" (Philem. 23–24).

And in Paul's final note to Timothy, perhaps just weeks before his execution, he has this request:

"Get Mark and bring him with you, because he is helpful to me in my ministry" (2 Tim. 4:11).

But the greatest evidence of John Mark's restoration is still to come. It is he—the undependable one—who records the second of the four gospels, an exciting, action-packed account of the life of our Lord. His place in history is thus assured forever.

If there is hope for John Mark, there is hope for us today. Few of us have squandered as much potential as he. His story, tucked into corners of the New Testament, is an inspiring example of starting again.

And it is inspiration, the glimmer of hope, of expectation, that we desperately need in the aftermath of our own stumblings. The Bible has more to say about hope than we have realized. We have been caught up with more impressive things. "And now abideth faith, hope, love, these three; but the greatest of these is love" (see 1 Cor. 13:13).

If love is the greatest . . . which is the least?

It is hope.

Hope is not strong enough to reach out to others, as love does. Hope can never move mountains—that requires genuine faith. Hence, we brush hope aside as minor, auxiliary, an extra. We don't hear many sermons about it. We don't write songs in its honor.

What is hope, anyway?

It is a quiet voice that says, "Maybe . . ." It softly reminds us that there is a faint possibility of a comeback.

Hope is actually very close to fear. Fear looks at a set of grim prospects and says, "It might fail." Hope looks at the same set of grim prospects . . . and says, "It might work."

Hope and fear are thus like two ships passing in the night, but headed in opposite directions. They are at the same dark, murky point in the ocean. But by morning, they will be miles apart.

Because hope keeps saying, "Well, *it's possible.*" Hope just may blossom someday into something impressive like faith. That is why Hebrews 11:1 defines faith as "being sure of what we hope for." In the beginning we are not sure at all. We know too well that it is ridiculous to put hope in ourselves. We have already demonstrated our own shortcomings. We can only hope that God is wise enough to make something beautiful out of our messed-up lives. We can only recognize that *it's possible.* At some future point we may be sure that he can and will, and that's faith. But for now . . .

I sat talking with a man in his fifties who had broken the chains of alcoholism nineteen years before and has worked with other alcoholics ever since. "Where do you begin?" I asked.

"The first step is to restore confidence," he answered readily. "Everything else must wait until the problem drinker is led to see that he or she just might make it this time. I tell them my story; I give them God's promises; I introduce them to other ex-alcoholics who have conquered—all to make that first crucial point. Once there's hope, we're on our way."

Jonathan, son of King Saul in the Old Testament, shows us what can happen to a hopeful attitude. In 1 Samuel 14, he and his father's army are in a desperate situation. The Philistines have five times as many chariots as Saul has *men*; his troops have dwindled to a mere six hundred. Saul can't make up his mind what to do; his options are severely restricted. The Philistines have long ago seized all the Israelite blacksmiths, leaving the army with almost no usable weaponry. The cold fact is that they are now simply waiting to die.

Does Jonathan stand and rally his father's men with an impassioned speech full of faith?

No. He can only muster a scrap of hope. He turns to one other person, his young armor-bearer, and suggests going over to the Philistine outpost. Why?

"Perhaps the LORD will act in our behalf. Nothing can hinder the LORD from saving, whether by many or by few" (1 Sam. 14:6).

Notice, he's making no predictions. He's simply stating a fact: *It's possible.*

The two young men gingerly let themselves be seen by the swaggering Philistines. "Come up to us and we'll teach you a lesson," the guards shout. Before the day is over, it is the other way around; the Israelites have won a stunning victory.

That's what hope can do, given a chance to grow. People in trouble often say, "I don't want to get my hopes up." Yes! Get them up! The Scripture promises in Romans 5:5 that "hope does not disappoint us, because God has poured out his love into our hearts by the Holy Spirit, whom he has given us." We have good reason to hope. If God is the kind of God he said he was in the previous section of this book, then we are quite justified in being hopeful. Romans 8:22–24 even goes so far as to describe God's intention to redeem us from this world of groaning and pain and then says: "For in this hope we were saved." Salvation is ours on so slender a platform as hope? Yes. Because hope is another word for confidence, and confidence in the Savior's work is all that is required.

A speaker named Doug Wead (whose sermon inspired much of this chapter) teases his audiences occasionally by asking, "Do you know what my favorite verse in all of Scripture is? It's none of the great classics—John 3:16, the Twenty-third Psalm, etc. My favorite, believe it or not, is Ecclesiastes 9:4." And then he quotes:

"Anyone who is among the living has hope—even a live dog is better off than a dead lion!"

He always draws a laugh, but his point is serious. More of us identify with dogs than with lions. We don't expect to be kings of the modern jungle. Yet even dogs can have hope.

Jesus spent most of his ministry reaching out to people who were sick, mistaken, unsure, a disappointment to themselves, tired. He did so, Matthew explains, to fulfill Isaiah's prophecy:

> *A bruised reed he will not break,*
> *and a smoldering wick he will not snuff out,*
> *till he leads justice to victory.*
> *In his name the nations will put their hope.*
>
> Matthew 12:20–21

Can we recover our balance after we have fallen? Can the pieces be put together again? Can we smile again, laugh again, love again? Can we, like John Mark, ever regain a place of usefulness?

It's possible.

For Your Reflection

1. People sometimes belittle hope as not being productive; they consider it a waste of time. How would you answer that?

2. Which hopes of yours have been shattered in the past? Were they hopes based on human beings, or hopes based on what God might do?

3. Spend some time meditating on Lamentations 3:19–33. What does this passage mean to you personally?

The phone rang on a cloudy Tuesday afternoon in the Walgreen's pharmacy department. The young brunette in the green sweater picked it up as she glanced out the window onto Denver's East Colfax Avenue.

"Hello, Pharmacy."

"Yes, this is Karen in Dr. Joel Martin's office. I have another patient prescription for you, please. This one's for Betty Schuman, S-C-H-U-M-A-N; give her a 30 count of Librium 10 milligrams, dosage twice a day with food."

The pharmacist's assistant cocked the phone against her left shoulder as she quickly scribbled down the instructions on a prescription pad.

"Got it. We'll take care of it," she replied and then hung up.

What the assistant had no way of knowing was that the voice on the other end of the line was not coming from someone in a white nurse's outfit in a medical office. It was instead a lawyer's wife and mother of three wearing jeans and a sweatshirt in her family room in the suburbs, a one-time x-ray technician who knew the medical protocols well. In her desperation for more tranquilizers, she was willing to commit a Class IV felony by calling in yet another phony "'script."

In a few hours, Sandy Bolte would get in her car and drive to Walgreen's. Nonchalantly edging up to the counter, she would say, "Prescription for Schuman, please—Betty Schuman." And in less than three minutes, with a quick forged signature and an exchange of cash, she would be on her way with yet another vial of powerful narcotics to keep her nerves subdued and her composure in place.

Sandy had been doing this for several months, ever since the doctor had cut off her long-running love affair with tranquilizers and muscle relaxants that had started back in her late twenties. A broken back and subsequent surgery to fuse the vertebrae at age twenty-one had left her vulnerable. Then, when as a newlywed her first two children had come along less than a year apart, "I was hit with terrific back spasms and pain," she says. "So the narcotics were justified at first. Over the years, the back problem gradually went away—but the pills continued."

Sandy's husband was Dennis, a comfortably paid government attorney. Sandy got to stay at home and do what she loved: raising her kids, volunteering at their school, fixing up her home, teaching Sunday school at the Presbyterian church, going to women's Bible studies. "With cute little Denise and Dennis Jr.—we called him DJ—we looked like the ideal family. And I guess we were—at least it appeared that way. When Christopher came along about eight years later, the picture was complete.

"What I didn't know, however, was what the Librium and the Fiorinal with codeine were doing to me. This second combination, by the way, is so strong it has since been taken off the market. My feelings were numbed; I didn't know my true emotions for all that time. I hadn't cried in who knows how long."

Sandy was into her early forties, with two children growing into teenagers, when something happened to uncover the masquerade. She developed a bleeding ulcer. Her doctor analyzed the various factors and came to the belated realization that this calm-looking housewife and mother was in fact addicted to the medication she had been taking now for sixteen years. He ordered her into a thirty-day residential treatment program to wean her off the drugs.

"What nobody told me," Sandy remembers, "is that it would be years before I'd be any sort of normal again. I began seeing a psychiatrist. All of a sudden I was very, very,

very depressed, even suicidal. It was awful. The bottom dropped out of my life."

Sandy knew one way to relieve her malaise, of course. The soothing medicine was still waiting at any corner pharmacy. That's when she began faking prescriptions, sometimes in writing, at other times over the phone. And harried pharmacists were too busy to check the validity of her orders.

"In an odd sort of way," she admits, "writing the 'scripts was almost as addictive as the drugs themselves. It was a challenge to pull off, an exciting adventure to see if I could get away with it yet another time."

With no limits on access, Sandy's intake began to climb. Before long she was gulping down fifteen to twenty pills at a time, four to five times a day. Her spree lasted ten months, until a diligent pharmacist finally happened to check back with the doctor to confirm what Sandy had requested. The charade suddenly came apart as police knocked on the door of the Bolte home.

Sandy found herself in court, embarrassed, ashamed, repentant. She told the judge she had made a big mistake and pleaded for leniency. He handed down a deferred sentence of one year, provided Sandy would go back into drug rehabilitation treatment. She eagerly agreed.

"I had a perfect chance to straighten up," she says. "If I would stay out of trouble for a year, my record would be wiped clean.

"But that didn't happen."

Not long after finishing the drug program, Sandy returned home—and returned to her narcotics. At this point Dennis was losing patience. "In years past, I'd always been the steady one in the marriage," Sandy says, "making most of the day-to-day decisions at home so he could just work.

Now I couldn't do that anymore, and he let me know I'd better shape up or ship out.

"I went into psychotherapy again. I urged him to come along with me, but after a couple of joint appointments, he said he didn't want to do that anymore.

"I was in no state to function. I kept downing huge doses of pills and was in and out of treatment programs for the next year. Meanwhile, the home was just totally unraveling."

Sandy was losing hope. Her extended family was unable to help. The church seemed not to know what to do with her. Communication with Dennis had shut down. She still remembers their last conversation, when she asked in dismay, "What are we going to do—just let the attorneys sort it out?"

His reply: "Yeah."

Soon thereafter, Sandy left home for good. She set up her own apartment. As the silence and the loneliness bore down on her, she found solace, of course, only in more drugs. And again, she got caught.

This time the sentence was more severe. She was placed in "Community Corrections" for eight months—a program in which the offenders must live in an old motel under watchful surveillance, keeping a curfew, but have permission to hold down a daytime job. "It's your last chance before prison," Sandy says. "I functioned really well for a while. My job, in fact, was working in a Christian bookstore!

"But when they let me return to my own home, I started using tranquilizers and painkillers again. I had no purpose in life. Somehow in all this upheaval, I had lost myself. I had little or no self-esteem. I didn't know who I was. The Lord I thought I knew, I didn't know intimately. I hadn't surrendered all that I was to him.

"I flunked out one more time, and that was it for the judge: He sentenced me to eighteen months at CWCF—the Colorado Women's Correctional Facility in Canon City."

The former suburbanite cried for five straight days in the county's interim processing center, shaking with panic at what lay ahead for her. She was about to be locked up with fist-swinging brawlers and aggressive lesbians; she knew she was doomed. "You'll never survive," more than one person told her. "They'll kill you before you know what hit you."

There was no postponing the inevitable, however. The day came that Sandy was driven 120 miles southwest from the Denver area to the small, mountain-ringed town of Canon City. The beauty of the snow-capped Rockies stood in silent contrast to the gray ugliness of her institutional future. She knew she had blown half a dozen opportunities to straighten up and avoid this fate.

"It's a whole revelation to walk through those gates and hear them clang shut behind you. You've lost everything. You can do absolutely nothing without asking permission—even going to the bathroom.

"You have to get up at 5:45 in order to eat breakfast at 6:00 and then be at your job at 7:00. Mine was ground maintenance. You get off work at 3:30 in the afternoon. That means lots of time to do nothing but put up with loud rap music.

"The homosexuality was quite obvious, although there were many of us who were not gay. One of my cells was right next to a lesbian couple, which was an awful situation. Another time I had a lesbian cellmate myself.

"Somehow, though, the Lord protected me. Nothing ever happened to me. They knew I claimed to be a Christian, and that's not a popular thing in prison. You get a lot of ridicule. But they never threatened me physically. Of course, I was fifty years old and white, while most of the others were in their twenties and minority. So I wasn't of any particular value to them in their peer groups." As for fights between inmates, Sandy saw only one during her time in prison.

A local woman named Jan came to lead a Bible study every Sunday night for about ten inmates. "I'd never look people in the eye," Sandy says, "and she'd come over, pull up my chin, and say, 'I love you, and the Lord loves you. You're a worthwhile person.' She did this over and over.

"Finally it began to click. *Maybe she's right. Maybe I didn't commit the unforgivable sin. Maybe God still loves me.*"

On Mother's Day, Jan said to the group, "Let's have a time of prayer now for all our kids."

"I don't pray for my kids," Sandy fired back. She had totally turned off the notion of family; she had no idea what Denise, DJ, and Christopher were even doing these days. As for her ex-husband, she knew he had quickly remarried.

Further than that, Sandy assumed God couldn't care less about any kind of prayer from her, even for innocent children.

Jan jumped to respond to Sandy's brush-off. "Oh, you must!" she said. "Even in prison, you have to ask God to watch over your kids." Soon the circle of women began lifting up names of children in sincere intercession.

When six months had passed, Sandy was eligible for parole. Because she had behaved herself, the officials told her she would be released to go back to Denver.

Sandy wasn't so sure she *wanted* out. "I'm not gonna make this," she told the parole office.

"But they didn't believe me. Although I had come closer to the Lord, I knew something still wasn't right; I wasn't strong enough to stay clean. So I went back to Denver—and within two months, I'd violated the parole and was back in the Denver County Jail."

Sandy's parole officer came to see her and viewed the situation as just a minor lapse. "Well, now, we'll get you out of here, and you can resume your parole," he said.

Sandy's face grew serious. "No, you don't understand," she replied. "Send me back to prison. That's my only salvation."

So back to Canon City she went, to finish out her full sentence. This time, the spiritual awakening that had been started before took full root. During the next nine months or so, "I really did totally surrender to the Lord—every morning. It was a turning point at last. On the job outside doing groundskeeping work, I spent a lot of time down on my knees—praying and crying to the Lord, saying, *If I ever get out of here again, something has to change within me.*"

Jan would write original Bible studies just for Sandy. She would also send her mail during the week—the only mail Sandy ever received. In time Sandy got a new cellmate who was warm and supportive, who insisted that both of them go regularly to Sunday chapel meetings and also do their Bible studies.

"It was during these days that I began to claim Jeremiah 29:11, that wonderful Scripture that says, "'For I know the plans I have for you,' declares the Lord, "plans to prosper you and not to harm you, plans to give you hope and a future.'" I would literally say those words every morning. I still do that today.

"When I walked out the gates the second time, I had no idea what God's plan might be. I didn't know if I'd ever get to see my kids again. There was no earthly reason to hope that I would . . . but then again, it wasn't totally impossible, was it?"

After a brief stay in Denver, Sandy returned to Canon City once again, of her own free will this time, to see the town from a different perspective. She wanted to walk the sidewalks she had seen only from a cellblock window. She called Jan, who invited her to come stay with her for a brief period. On about the fifth day, the Lord seemed to say to Sandy, *You could move here, you know.*

So she did. Severing her ties with Denver, she found a modest place to live in Canon City and began a new life. Soon she got involved with a ministry called Prayer Warriors for Prisoners and also with the well-known Prison Fellowship outreach.

"I landed a job in home health care—which was a major error," she says. "Wouldn't you know that I'd be helping a patient in her home one day, and she offered me some Darvon! I fell once again.

"What a wake-up call! It scared the wits out of me. I enrolled in a monthlong outpatient treatment program and admitted to my employer what I'd done.

"Fortunately, they didn't fire me. They said that once I finished this latest program, I could have my old job back.

"I said, 'Thank you, but oh no—I need to get totally out of the medical field.' I knew in my heart that I had worked my last day in health care."

Sandy got a job at City Market on the cleaning crew. After a year and a half, she was promoted to assistant manager of the salad bar. Surrounded by nothing stronger than shredded lettuce and bacon bits, she goes to work each day determined to stay clean. "I suppose I could work in the pharmacy there," she says with a laugh, "but *no way!* I've had several discussions with the head pharmacist. He assures me they call back to verify all 'scripts."

When she gets a headache herself, she is extra cautious about what she takes. "My doctor knows all about my past, so he won't even give me cough medicine with codeine. Anything I take has to be nonnarcotic unless I'm in a hospital where they can monitor me.

"I've learned to be nice to my body and to rest a lot."

Along with the physical traces of the past, there are emotional scars as well. Sandy's daughter is still too wounded to speak to her mother. Sandy's middle son, DJ, has managed to cross the gulf, however. He showed up at the funeral of Sandy's mother, giving Sandy her first glimpse of him in more than a decade. No longer a squeaky-voiced adolescent, he had turned into a handsome young man.

"Now I talk to him on the phone from time to time," Sandy says. "He's very open and loving. He doesn't seem to want to talk about the past, however, so we don't. We just go on.

"I'm just grateful to be in touch once again."

When her youngest, Christopher, graduated from high school, Sandy was there—the only one of her three whom she got to see in a cap and gown. She had already begun to pray, *Lord, if it's your will, could I please have another chance with Christopher?* When he was little, the two of them had been very close. Now he seemed a little uncertain about his future. Should he go on to college? What should he do with his life?

Sandy took the risk of saying, "Christopher, you need to come live with me in Canon City and go to school. I'd really love to have you." He jumped at the chance. Sandy could hardly believe that God would give her a second opportunity with this special child.

"We're the best of friends," she says with a beaming face. "He's going to community college and thinks he might major in psychology. He tells me everything. I wonder how I got so blessed. It's like a little bit of heaven."

"I see his self-esteem growing by leaps and bounds. The Lord is really working in his life. He wants to be a man after God's own heart.

"We don't have much money, but if he has five dollars, he'll give it to me if I need it, and I do the same for him. So in another way, we're rich."

Mother and son have devotions together every morning and sit together in church on Sundays. Sandy knows she is belatedly impacting his life for good.

She's also having an influence on the lives of others. "I watch the moms with little kids as they come in to City Market, and I just look at them and think about what I missed. Then I silently pray for them."

Sandy leads a Tuesday afternoon Bible study for women at the county jail. More than one inmate has said, "What in the world makes you come back here? If I ever get out of here, I'm *never* coming back."

Sandy replies, "I'm here because the Lord sent me. He wants you to know there's a better life."

She goes home each week reveling in the fulfillment of passing along what she has learned the hard way, of telling others how they can make it. One afternoon, two of the women in the circle made open commitments to follow Christ.

Why did the Lord give Sandy Bolte a second chance?

"It's nothing that I did, that's for sure," she says. "It was just his unconditional love that picked me up, dusted me off, and said, 'Okay, try again. Maybe you can do things differently this time.'

"I just feel the Lord's presence so much when I pray or read the Scriptures these days. I'm not lonely anymore. He healed me of the loneliness even before Christopher came.

"He has restored me more than I ever dreamed could be possible."

If you were looking for seedbeds of adultery, you'd probably skip over the quiet river town of Prairie du Chien, Wisconsin.

Coal barges glide past on their way up the Mississippi toward La Crosse and on to Minneapolis. The townspeople lead generally wholesome Midwestern lives, and when Keith Govier was growing up, he went to church with his six brothers most Sundays of the year. The worst thing he ever did in high school was get caught riding in a stolen car one night. "I was on the edge of a bunch of questionable guys," he says with a shy smile. His blond hair and handsome appearance let you know that he couldn't have been much of a terror.

It was during his senior year that he and some friends walked to the front of the Wesleyan church during a revival meeting to make their professions of faith. "After that, some things definitely changed," Keith remembers. "I stopped swearing and running around and going to questionable places. Although I was following people's expectations to some degree, I had made at least a start to follow the Lord."

He worked a year after high school, then joined the Air Force, and by the age of nineteen had married his high school sweetheart. "Connie was Catholic, but she agreed to change over." When active military duty was finished, the young couple settled back in Prairie du Chien and worshiped regularly at first. Keith became a cop.

"I was working a lot of nights and weekends, and over the next three or four years, it was hard to get to church on Sunday morning. So she'd go on without me. Plus, in a town of only five thousand, the police know just about everybody's business. I found myself growing a bit cynical about church members to whose homes I'd be called to break up family arguments or drinking parties."

Old habits of speech and living began to return. Disagreements with Connie became more frequent, especially after a second pregnancy came along unplanned. Young Shawn had been one of the few delights of his life, but the thought of another newborn depressed him.

On the job, Keith would listen to his police partner tell about the various girlfriends he was enjoying. "Connie and I had waited for marriage," Keith says, "and I'd been faithful to her up to now, but I began to see what I was missing, and it looked appealing."

The turning point came in a discussion in the spring of 1979 when, after seven downhill years, Connie said she did not love him anymore. "That tore me apart," Keith remembers. "We had let a lot of problems build up unresolved, but that meant the end as far as I was concerned. If she didn't love me, I would find someone who did."

His affair over the next four months with the wife of a best friend brought physical pleasure, but it was not without misgivings. "I'd be alone in the patrol car at night, and I'd pray, 'Lord, I'm going to turn this all around. Please forgive me for what I've done. I'm going to stop.' The next morning, though, it was like I'd wake up, and Satan would say, 'You dummy, you know you can't do that.' And he was right."

Things came to a dramatic crisis when the woman decided to tell her husband she was leaving him. The news was suddenly all over town, and Keith felt he had no choice but to resign from the police force. His reputation had been smudged, and he had made himself all the more undesirable to Connie.

"But where was I going to find a new job in a small town?" He was soon on his way to Springfield, Illinois, to become a Montgomery Ward's security manager. He set up an apartment, and when he called home after two months to ask how it was going. Connie's reply was "Fine—couldn't be better."

His lover, however, never took up his invitation to come to Springfield for a visit; she was earnestly trying to rebuild her own marriage. In time, Keith dated three local girls, the last of whom impressed him with her high standards. "Nancy wasn't a born-again Christian, but she was very organized and responsible—all the things that were missing in my life. It bothered me that she could be so moral without faith."

Gradually, something inside Keith told him, *You need to go back to church*. He did so several times, but held himself at a distance. "I felt lots of guilt," he says, "and I assumed I needed to straighten myself up first *before* returning to God."

His sister-in-law, concerned about what was happening and believing that Keith needed to be confronted, drove down from Madison, Wisconsin, to see him. Over a two-hour dinner she grilled him about his priorities, his responsibility for two young children, and the folly of trying to succeed apart from God.

"She was tough on me—but we'd always had a good relationship, and I didn't resent her for what she said. I knew it was the truth. The trouble was, I was falling in love at the time, and I didn't want to give Nancy up.

"I couldn't make a decision. To be honest, I hadn't made any good decisions for a year. I'd just rolled with the punches as they came along, doing whatever was easiest at the moment. What I needed to realize was that indecision is a decision."

By December, Keith had been transferred to Niles, Ohio, a move that cooled the liaison back in Springfield. The financial noose was tightening around his neck as the cost of maintaining two households steadily drained his savings and forced the sale of such things as his boat. By the end of the month, word came from Wisconsin that a divorce suit had been filed.

"I was sitting alone in my bare apartment one winter afternoon with just a chair, a table, a TV, a bed, and not much else. I began watching a Christian program—I don't even remember which one. The longer I watched, the more I had to admit that I'd come to the end of the road. I knelt down and began to cry. 'Lord,' I prayed, 'here I am. I know I'm not much but a lot of trouble and a big stack of bills, but if you'll forgive me, you can use me however you like. I'm yours.'"

It was the beginning. An older woman at the Ward's store referred Keith to a church in nearby Warren, where for the next four months "I grew spiritually more than ever before. They set me on my feet and pointed me in the right direction very quickly."

Could the marriage be repaired at this late date? He sat down and wrote a long letter, admitting the wrong he had done, asking Connie's forgiveness, and telling excitedly about the change in his life. Days passed, with no response. When he finally called, the answer was cool. "Well, I've heard all that before. You brought me out of the Catholic church in the first place, remember? But look what's happened in spite of your religion."

Keith continued to pray regularly for a restoration, right up until the court date in June. He could not afford a lawyer, but he drove to Wisconsin and met with her attorney, agreeing to what amounted to about an 80/20 split of the assets. At the trial, the judge asked him the crucial question: "Do you consider this marriage irretrievably broken?"

"No, Your Honor, I don't," Keith replied. "A lot of things have changed in my life, and I think we can put it back together again."

A look of shock came across Connie's face. When he stepped down from the stand, she stood and approached him. "You never said that before!" she whispered.

"Well, maybe not in those words, but that's really how I feel," he replied.

Nevertheless, by the time the judge put the same question to Connie, her response was firm. "Yes, it is broken; there's no chance for repair." And the divorce was granted.

Keith returned to his work; by this time he'd landed a better-paying position as security director of a large shopping mall in Rockford, Illinois. But "after about two weeks, it hit me. Why had I given into everything so easily? Why had I taken on debts that should have been split 50/50? Why had I let her have the newer car while I drove the old junker, which was in desperate need of a valve job?

"I prayed not to feel animosity toward Connie. 'Lord, help me to stay away from the phone when I feel like telling her off.' After all, I was the one who cheated on her in the beginning, and her coldness toward my return to the Lord was understandable.

"The more I thought about my two kids growing up in a non-Christian environment, the more depressed I became. But the Lord seemed to assure me that he would meet my needs regardless. I kept reading the verse that had become real to me back in Ohio: 'Be strong and very courageous. Be careful to obey . . . do not turn from it to the right or to the left, that you may be successful wherever you go'" (Josh. 1:7).

God's kindness toward Keith was never more apparent than in the way his financial pressures were finally relieved. "We'd bought the house in Prairie du Chien through FHA, and after the divorce was final, their regulations required that the loan be rewritten in her name alone.

The paperwork took a while to process, but when it was all said and done, I received a check for my half of the equity.

"Suddenly the load was gone. I cleared up all the old debts and was even able to trade cars with the surplus!"

In the years since then, Keith Govier's life has stabilized; his bills are paid, his work is going well, and he's solidly involved in a growing church. His pastor initially gave him a vote of confidence by asking him to work with the boys' club that met on Wednesday nights; more responsibilities have come since.

The new era that began in his life is best expressed when he says, "I'm no longer a passive Christian. I want to learn more of the Word and to serve the Lord any way I can. The important thing in my life now is to concentrate on what will last."

The future is promising, not because Keith has done everything right in life so far, but because he's surrendered to the God who can handle imperfection.

The steps of a man are from the LORD . . .
though he fall, he shall not be cast headlong,
for the LORD is the stay of his hand.

Psalm 37:23–24 (RSV)

the need

for confrontation

facing
facts

An award-winning TV commercial for Alka-Seltzer once showed a middle-aged man in obvious distress after finishing off a large, well-topped pizza. As he clutched his middle, his wife stood by and reproachfully intoned, "You ate it, Ralph— you ate the *whole* thing."

Ralph could only stare into the camera and echo in a tomblike voice, "I can't believe I ate the whole thing."

There are times in our lives when we simply cannot find someone else to blame. We search the landscape in vain for another human being to indict. We say, "Well, it wasn't actually my fault, because . . ." and we can't finish the sentence.

In the past, we've been able to find alibis. There were circumstances that pushed us to do what we did. Older and more powerful persons misled us, gave us bad advice. Our problems were traceable to several sources, at least some of which were outside our control.

But this time, we can find no such cushioning. This is not a case of "It happened to me." This is a case of "I did it." We cannot sidestep the fact that the present predicament is of our own making, and to blame anyone else is but to prolong the self-deception.

We do not come to such an admission easily. It hurts too much. In fact, the various profiles in this book show that we often don't *come* to the ugly truth at all; we are dragged to it by outside forces. Circumstances gang up on us to such a degree that no other conclusion is possible; we must finally face the music. Only when the police move in, or a spouse explodes in enlightened rage, or the doctor confirms that a child is indeed on the way, must we grudgingly admit what has been going on.

What is sometimes hard for us to appreciate at this point is that there is more than just fate working against us. It is more than a matter of our luck running out. Behind the scenes, God is at work, quietly but irresistibly bringing us to his mirror. The events of our lives are his pressure bars, gradually nudging us where we would not go otherwise, until we are confronted with ourselves.

Why, after Jonah had rejected the instruction to go to Nineveh, did God not just let him proceed to a leisurely vacation in Tarshish? Jonah had made his decision; could not God move on to select another, more obedient prophet? Indeed, he could have done so, and with good justification.

But instead, he went to the bother of arranging a rather complicated set of phenomena. First "the LORD sent a great wind on the sea" (Jonah 1:4), and when that had sufficiently gotten Jonah's attention, "the LORD provided a great fish" (Jonah 1:17). The great wind and the great fish were effective; the prophet could no longer escape the fact that something was terribly wrong in his life.

The book of Genesis tells us about Jacob spending all night trying to get ready for a critical meeting with his brother, Esau.

Jacob has fought and scrapped to the point in life where he now has a growing family and flocks and herds, but his relationship with God is still sketchy. He comes to the Jabbok River and sends his caravan on across. Then in the darkness, all alone, he is accosted by a stranger.

They wrestle until daybreak, and when Jacob, exhausted, asks for a blessing, the stranger asks an odd but penetrating question:

"What is your name?"

It is almost as if the divine messenger is saying, "Jacob, what is your real problem? You've blamed your father, Isaac, for his favoritism toward Esau; you've blamed your brother for his sour attitude; you've blamed your Uncle Laban for his shadiness—but down at the root of things, *who are you*? You're Jacob—the supplanter, the tricky one. Face it!"

And in that moment, God worked a fundamental change in Jacob's nature. He even gave the man a new name, Israel. His life from that night on had a different tone of sensitivity to his Lord, with the results that greater peace and happiness came his way.

Why does God force us to confront who we are and what we have done? Does he not know how painful it is for us? Does he enjoy embarrassing us, devastating our self-respect, watching us grovel in shame before him and everyone else who knows us?

Not at all. But God is wise enough to know that pain is the greatest motivator to change. It is a sad fact, but a true one. People change faster when they *hurt* than under almost any other condition. Any parent of a toddler will verify that sometimes words don't work; only a spanking gets the message through. It is not much different with adults.

Almost fifty years ago the famous Lutheran speaker Walter A. Maier told his radio audience:

> This, then, is the purpose of pain for the redeemed:
> it is one of your Father's ways of speaking to you; it is the

evidence of His limitless love, by which He would draw you farther from evil and closer to Him, the blessed means by which He would hold you back from sin, but hold you up to grace, the divine remedy which can cure you of pride and help you lean more trustingly on the Lord.[1]

So long as we do not perceive that we "really did eat the whole thing," so long as we are not aware of our willfulness, we are not likely to turn to the One who forgives and restores. God has a great fund of patience for us, but he will get to the bare facts eventually. "If we claim to be without sin," says 1 John 1:8, "we deceive ourselves and the truth is not in us."

Have you ever wondered why God dealt so harshly with Ananias and Sapphira in the early church, while other liars in the Bible (Abram and David, for example) seemed to get off much easier? Perhaps it was because Ananias and Sapphira refused to crumple when faced with the evidence; they kept up their pretension of righteousness even after Peter's question. They thus were an exhibit of Pharisaism, something Jesus hated almost more than anything else. He was determined not to let his church become infected with that virus. He stamped it out immediately.

In contrast, Jonah prayed honestly from inside the fish; Jacob admitted the kind of man he was; David poured out his heart in the Fifty-first Psalm and others. They yielded to the inexorable searchlight that bore down upon them.

One of the benefits of facing the facts is that we are then released from a great deal of tension. As Don Osgood notes in his book *Pressure Points*, "It reduces stress to admit we're wrong."[2] While our external dilemma may remain, our internal state has definitely improved. We know where we stand.

A woman who eventually worked as an editor with a Christian publishing company told of leaving home at the age of sixteen to get married. She could hardly wait to escape the confines of her family and the negative church in her small town. She and her young husband set up their home a safe distance away, and two children were born in the first three years. But the rebellion within her kept surfacing, and the marriage soon split.

"Here I was, nineteen years old, with two kids to support," she said from the vantage point of nearly three decades later. "I headed for the West Coast, blaming other people and other things for my troubles. But eventually I had to realize that *I* had made the choices. My life was a mess because of what I had elected to do with it."

She eventually remarried, began sending her children to Sunday school, and finally started going with them. By the age of twenty-four, her relationship with God had been repaired, and a useful adulthood was underway.

Alcoholics Anonymous has for years asked men and women to state that they have a problem out of control, a situation they cannot handle alone. Experience has shown that something crucial happens in that admission, something that unlocks the door to genuine change.

And change is what God is about in the end. He has no desire to fry us in the heat of exposure; he means to bring us to a new day. In fact, he may even have a surprise up his sleeve that will make positive use of our pain. The forty-year-old Moses, in a moment of outrage, committed murder. In that instant, his future as Pharaoh's protégé was forever lost. He fled in terror to the Midian desert, there to contemplate the wreckage of his career.

But God began to restore him, and eventually commissioned him at a burning bush. His years of living in that rugged terrain were not a waste, for one day he would return to the same wilderness as the leader of a migration. His place of retreat would become his place of honor. The former murderer would become the man of God.

The unmasking of ourselves is a necessary part of God's process of healing. We must endure its pain and look forward to the relief that will surely follow.

For Your Reflection

1. Try to describe your life situation or difficulty using sentences that start with "I ..." Reject any sentences that describe what other people or groups of people have done. Strive to name what is your responsibility.

2. Are there pressures forcing you to face reality, to lay aside the various explanations you've used in the past? What might God be trying to teach you through these pressures?

"God does not take away life; instead, he devises ways so that a banished person may not remain estranged from him."

—2 Samuel 14:14

In this excerpt from his book Where Eagles Soar, *well-known author and speaker Jamie Buckingham described how God painfully confronted him with a sin—not once but twice. He was a successful pastor in his mid-thirties at the time, but only after this canyon of embarrassment did his wider ministry as a writer emerge.*

Exposure comes, not for the sake of punishment, but for the sake of salvation. Fortunate is the man who is exposed early in life. Pity the man who is smart enough to hide his sin until the judgment.

Etched forever in my memory are the events that took place the night of exposure. Like Jacob at Peniel, I wrestled— and lost. October 1965. I sat in the beautiful conference room of that large Baptist church in South Carolina, surrounded by a group of twenty deacons, all with stern faces. They had tried over the last few months to convince me to resign. They knew something was wrong but until this dreadful night had found no evidence. As the months of suspicion continued, I hung on. To leave would mean admission of guilt. Worse, it would mean leaving behind a relationship in which I reveled with the same degree of intensity an alcoholic does with his bottle.

Twice before I had stood before the church at the monthly business meeting and gone through a "vote of confidence." Twice I had bluffed my way through. But this time there was concrete evidence. One of the deacons had discovered a note. I had been laid bare. My insides were churning. Desperately I tried to hold the façade of false confidence.

They asked me to leave the meeting and wait outside as they discussed the matter. Instead of at least a pretense at a sedate exit, I bolted. Fled. I stumbled into the darkened sanctuary and knelt at the front, weeping in fear and confusion. Back in the conference room the men were deciding my fate. In the next room was a small office. I called Jackie. "Come get me. I can't take it anymore." I hung up and in a state of near shock, shamed and faced with the awfulness of it all, I wandered down a flight of stairs lit dimly by only the quiet redness of an exit light.

She found me, the shepherd of the flock, crouched in a fetal position in a basement hallway, huddled against the landing of the stairs. "It would be better for you, for the children, for this church if I were dead," I sobbed.

She comforted. She soothed. She never asked for details. There was no need. She led me by the hand through the dark hallways of the house of God to our car parked under the lighted window of the conference room. I did not realize it at the time, but those men were God's servants—sent by the Holy Spirit to perform the unpleasant task of shaking a man of God until only the unshakable remained.

That night I walked into the front yard of our beautiful parsonage. Standing under the autumn sky, I looked up into the heavens and screamed: "Take me! Take me now! Quickly!" In a desperate move, I grabbed my shirt and ripped it open at the chest, tearing the buttons and hem as I exposed my bare chest to the heavens, waiting for the inevitable flash of lightning which I knew would come and split me asunder, carrying me into the hell where I belonged.

But there was no flash of lightning, for the purging fire had already begun to burn. And besides, God does not punish sin the way we punish it. As ranchers burn off a pasture to kill the weeds so the new grass can sprout, so the consuming fire of God burns away the dross without consuming the sinner.

There was more to follow, of course. For one thing, we had to leave. Then there was the fear of going to sleep at night because I could not stand the thought of waking to a new day. Better to sit up sleepless nights than sleep and start a new day without trumpets in the morning. There was the desperate reaching out for friends, only to find they had all deserted. I was like a leper. Unclean. I wrote letters—more than ninety of them—to pastoral and denominational friends. Only one man dared respond and that was with a curt, "I received your letter and shall be praying for you."

Perhaps God was working here too; comfort or encouragement at that agonizing time could have moved me even deeper into a continuing self-deceiving sense of feeling justified.

And anyway, what else could anyone say?

We returned to my home state of Florida, to a small but rapidly growing church—the only opportunity that was open. But as Vance Havner once remarked, it doesn't do any good to change labels on an empty bottle. Nothing inside me had changed. I was still the magnificent manipulator, the master of control, the defender of my position. I was still pushing people around. I was far more politician than a man of God. The Holy Spirit was not controlling my life.

Soon echoes from the past began drifting down to Florida—rumors of adultery, of manipulation, of lying. The old undertow of fear sucked at my guts. I was about to be swept back to sea, for I had not been honest with the committee which had interviewed me for the Florida position. I could feel the insidious inevitability of confrontation creeping upon me again. I continued to fight, to brave the growing onslaught of fact that kept building the case against me. It took fifteen months of a stormy relationship before the Florida church cast me into the waves to calm the sea— just like Jonah.

The crisis exploded one Sunday morning when I stepped up to the pulpit to preach. On the pulpit stand was a petition asking me to resign. It was signed by 350 people, many of whom were sitting, smiling, in the congregation. A group of men had hired a private detective and checked into my past. The detective's report—all forty-seven pages of badly distorted facts—had been duplicated and handed out to the congregation. The deacons demanded I take a lie detector test. Even though I passed it—declaring I had no intention of perpetrating upon that new church the sins of my past—it was not enough. I had no choice but once again to slink home and huddle with my wife and children while the fire of God continued its purging work.

Often, I have discovered, we cannot hear God when we are busy. Hearing comes only when we have taken—or are forced to take—times of quietness. With Moses it took forty years of wandering in the burning sands of the Sinai, tending the sheep and goats of Jethro, his father-in-law and the priest of Midian, on the backside of the desert. It took that long for the fire of God to purge him of all the pride of his Egyptian prestige. Only then was he able to hear. Only then, when everything was quiet, did the angel of the Lord appear in the flame of fire out of the midst of the bush which burned but was not consumed. When a man has many things to do, he often does not have time to turn aside and see great sights. His time is consumed with busyness, his mind with activity. But Moses had time. So when the bush burned on the side of Mt. Horeb, he left his grazing flock and climbed the side of the rocky mountain to investigate. Then it was that God spoke to him and gave him direction.

So it was with me. All activity had ceased. No longer did I have to attend important committee meetings. No longer did I have to supervise budgets, direct visitation programs, promote an attendance campaign or even prepare sermons. All that I had felt was important was taken from me.

There was nothing to do but tend the few sheep and goats who had pulled out of the church with me and were huddled together on the hillside grazing. I was beyond my own control. Then my bush burned.

Someone, perhaps my mother, had entered a subscription in my name for *Guideposts* magazine. I seldom read *Guideposts*, but in my idle time, which I now had in great abundance, I picked it up. Someplace in that particular issue I found a half-page announcement of a writers' workshop to be sponsored by the magazine. The stipulations were simple. Submit a first-person manuscript of 1,500 words following the basic *Guideposts* style. This would be evaluated and judged by an editorial committee who would then pick the best twenty manuscripts. Those selected would receive an all-expense-paid trip to New York and would attend a one-week writers' workshop, conducted by the magazine editors, at the Wainwright House at Rye, New York, on Long Island Sound.

Several years before I had befriended a young man who was preparing to go to South America as a missionary pilot with a group known as the Jungle Aviation and Radio Service, the flying arm of the Wycliffe Bible Translators. I had been intrigued with Tom Smoak's story. . . . Since I had nothing else to do, I wrote the story and sent it in.

My bush burned on October 1, 1967. I was stretched out on the bed in the back room of our little rented house when the phone rang. It was from Leonard LeSourd, editor of *Guideposts*, stating I was one of the twenty winners—out of more than 2,000 submissions.

. . . At the workshop John and Elizabeth Sherrill, both editors for *Guideposts* at the time, were approached by Dan Malachuk, a book publisher who was looking for a writer to compose the story of Nicky Cruz. Nicky was a former

Puerto Rican gang leader from New York, now a Pentecostal preacher, whose conversion had played a major part in *The Cross and the Switchblade*, the book John and Elizabeth had written with David Wilkerson. The Sherrills were not interested in the project but recommended me. Before the week was out I had signed an agreement with the publisher and was on my way back to Egypt with a new sense of direction. I was going to become a writer. . . .

Perfection still eludes me. I am still vulnerable. But most important, I am no longer satisfied with my imperfection. Nor, thank God, am I intimidated by it. I have reached the point of recognizing that God uses imperfect, immoral, dishonest people. In fact, that's all there are these days. All the holy men seem to have gone off and died. There's no one left but us sinners to carry on the ministry.

Come, let us return to the LORD.
He has torn us to pieces
but he will heal us;
he has injured us
but he will bind up our wounds.
After two days he will revive us;
on the third day he will restore us,
that we may live in his presence.

Hosea 6:1–2

Search me, O God, and know my heart;
test me and know my anxious thoughts.
See if there is any offensive way in me,
and lead me in the way everlasting.

Psalm 139:23–24

When you're the fourth-born in a family of five, it's hard to stake out your individuality. And when you're the only girl among four brothers, it's even harder to compete for attention.

Amy Robnik found a way, however. A very dubious way.

By junior high she had decided that the Christianity she had grown up with wasn't everything it claimed to be. If it were, how come her parents didn't get along better? They took the family to church every Sunday and Wednesday night, but somehow it didn't seem to help their marriage very much.

And another thing: How come her dad lost his job as a computer programmer, and the only new ones he could find were out of town? That meant his leaving their northern Minnesota town of Esko early Monday morning, and Amy wouldn't see him again until late Friday night—just when she was at the age of needing him most.

"I didn't get along with my mom at all," the energetic blonde now admits. "I became very rebellious. Yes, I'd accepted the Lord as my Savior back when I was eight years old, but it was mainly a fear thing, at the end of one of those scary Christian movies about the Tribulation. I didn't understand much about a relationship with God, in spite of all the Sunday school classes I'd been in."

Amy began dating early. The first boyfriend was not a Christian, although she remembers him as a fairly moral person. Soon there were others, and by age sixteen she was seriously contemplating having sex. Why not? The idea of marriage was not all that attractive, after seeing her parents' example. Hardly any of Amy's friends at school, either girls or guys, were still virgins.

"But at the same time, I remember feeling that God sort of said if I'd wait until marriage, he would bless me with a husband who was a virgin, and I'd have a happy future. That made me feel warm and peaceful inside, like, *Wow, that would be awesome, if I could only keep up my end of the bargain.*"

She did not, however. Amy's early sexual experiences made her feel somewhat obligated to the boyfriend, and when he said he was going to stay in nearby Duluth, Amy found herself torn. She wanted to get away from home to a distant college as soon as possible. Reluctantly she broke up with him.

Amy's self-destructive behavior increased. "As soon as I turned eighteen, I moved out of the house to my best friend's house. Things really went downhill fast. I was drinking, and I was hurting. Friends tried to tell me, 'Amy, you have a problem. You're an alcoholic.' But I wouldn't listen."

The summer after high school graduation, yet another dating relationship hit the rocks, and in a troubled frame of mind, Amy headed off to a Christian college in the Twin Cities that fall. She was in no mood to benefit from its atmosphere, while she quickly exploited its freedoms. "I just went crazy. I stopped going to church, now that no one was forcing me. I was drinking a lot already, and I found other kids who would join me.

"A lot of them would party with me on the weekends and then pretend they didn't know me in school because they wanted to be seen as 'angels.' I was so turned off. I'd expound about Christian hypocrites. I've always been the kind of person who's exactly what you see; I'm not going to try to fake you out."

By the end of the first year, Amy concluded that the Christian campus was not the place for her. Where else could she go and be her real self? How about far, far away from Minnesota? That fall found Amy in the Deep South, at Auburn University in Alabama. Here there was no need even to think about Christianity. Alcohol was abundant, and so were drugs. She quickly found a crowd that made her comfortable.

"The more I drank, the more I lost my values and the more I slept around. I made more and more mistakes," she says today with sadness. "Some of that baggage is still with me, in fact. There were some close calls at times with drug dealers, but I always managed to escape."

She had enough natural talent to keep making good grades. This helped her rationalize: *I'm not an alcoholic. Alcoholics are bums. They don't make A's like I'm doing.*

Amy actively pursued friendships with black students, who were more plentiful than back in Minnesota. It became another part of her self-differentiation, her venture across lines that others would hesitate to broach. While many of her African-American friends were avid partygoers, there was also a Christian girl named Annie who became a close soulmate. "We talked a lot. She showed me so much love. She knew everything I was doing, but she never condemned me or wrote me off. She would just ask me innocent questions, like 'Amy, have you prayed recently?'"

The fast life continued in her junior year of college, and with the coming of her twenty-first birthday on November 4, she was now totally legal to enter any bar—although being underage had seldom stopped her up to this point. She looked forward to this day as her final emancipation.

At the same time, Amy had to admit that her reckless behavior was getting a little old. Nothing seemed to make her feel fulfilled. She was depressed, at times almost suicidal. She told Annie about her inner doubts and then blurted out as a last resort, "What if I went to church with you sometime?"

Annie smiled and said yes, of course. They arranged that on the following Sunday they would get up early and drive two hours south to Annie's home church near Ozark, Alabama, not far from the Florida panhandle.

The Saturday night before, Amy went out drinking with some friends. Around one o'clock in the morning the thought hit her inebriated brain, *I really should go home now. I have to get up early in the morning to go to church!*

The alarm clock went off at six o'clock, and Amy reluctantly rolled out of bed. She lit a cigarette to try to jumpstart her body. All too soon, Annie and another friend were knocking on her door, smiling and ready to start the day's journey. Amy greeted them with a grunt, then crawled into the car and slept most of the way.

When she awakened at last, around nine o'clock, she found herself approaching a small all-black holiness church in the country, with green fields on every side. The sky was beautifully clear. "I looked up at the white steeple and thought, *Okay, here we go. Whatever. . . .*

"Inside, I was the only white face in the building. And I was definitely the only person in jeans and a sweater! Every other woman in the place wore a Sunday dress and her hair in a bun, it seemed. The man teaching adult Sunday school wore a white suit.

"An hour later, the worship service began. The music had all the soul you would expect in such a place. The preacher wore a long robe, and his sermon quickly fell into the classic sing-song rhythm. I don't remember his text— only his manner: He was very loving. I was entranced.

"Somewhere in the middle of his sermon, he sort of interrupted himself and said, 'Somebody needs to come forward to this altar right now.' Bam! I was up and on my feet, hardly realizing I was moving."

Women of the congregation soon gathered around the scruffy college student, imploring God to move into her heart and wash it clean at last. Amy remembers the occasion almost in surreal terms. Time stood still. "I was calling out to the Lord, and people kept saying to me, 'Just receive, honey, just receive.' The pinnacle verse in that denomination, I guess, is Acts 2:38—'Repent and be baptized, every one of you, in the name of Jesus Christ for the forgiveness of your sins. And you will receive the gift of the Holy Spirit.' That's what I wanted."

To let the service proceed to its natural conclusion, the deaconesses guided Amy toward a side room to continue praying. She remembers at one point the sensation of a big white light.

And then the women, with all warmth and love, began to say, "If you really want the Lord to come live within you, there are some things you need to let go. Just confess them to God. Go ahead and repent."

Amy didn't have trouble thinking of things. First on the list was unforgiveness toward her mother. Then came her sexual life. Next was drinking. One by one, she spelled out her sins to God and agreed to give them up. The scene was emotional and tearful, but underneath there was genuine penitence, too.

"I basically dealt with everything I knew I should," she says, "—except cigarettes. I was too hooked to bring up that subject."

Hours flew by, and the morning turned into afternoon. The praying continued. "They were telling me to open up to the Holy Spirit, the Comforter. I kind of knew what they meant, but then when words and syllables I didn't understand came tumbling out of my mouth, I knew this had to be God. He was taking over every part of me, even my speech."

At last everyone stood up for a round of fervent hugs. The minister's wife exhorted her, "Here's your key word, Amy: faith, faith, faith. You're a new creation. You walk by faith now. You're not the same person you were when you got up this morning."

Then she followed with "Would you like to be baptized today? You really should." Amy nodded her head as she wiped away her tears.

The service had been dismissed, but the families of the women who had been praying with Amy were still around. In a few minutes, she entered the baptistery and was immersed as a sign of her new life in Christ.

"I remember how all the little black kids were fascinated with watching this white girl go down into the water and come back up again!" she says with a laugh. "But more than that, the baptism showed how my old self was dying and my new self was coming alive. I'm glad they insisted."

Then right at the end, one of the ladies came back to Amy and said in a low voice, "Before I leave, I have to ask you this: Do you smoke?"

After a little fudging, Amy admitted the truth.

"Well, God says, 'No more,'" the woman replied. "You're going to be a Christian now."

Inside Amy felt like, *Oh, man, do I really have to give up cigarettes on top of everything else? How can I ever manage this?*

It was 3:30 in the afternoon when Amy finally came out of that little church into the sunshine. It had been an overwhelming day. As she crawled back into the car for the return trip to Auburn, she was a little confused on some doctrinal points, but she knew what had happened was real. Her memory flashed back to how drunk she had been just the night before, and she knew God had now filled her with his Spirit to empower her for overcoming those things. Otherwise, she was sure her turnaround would not last.

"When I walked back into my apartment that evening, there were my pajamas still lying on the bathroom floor from the morning shower. I stared at them. In an odd sort of way, they symbolized the old me, now discarded for something far better. I was a new person.

"I'd never thought I was good enough to be a Christian. Now I was cleansed, forgiven, and headed onto a new road altogether."

Giving up cigarettes was every bit as hard as Amy had feared. "They were like my pacifier. Sometimes I'd literally shake with 'nic-fits,' wanting them so bad. One time I was on my way out the door to buy a pack, and at the same time I was praying, 'God! You've got to do something right now!' Somehow he stopped me."

Annie and her friends began urging her to strengthen her new faith by attending campus Bible studies. There they helped sharpen the picture of what it would take to please God. "You can't go back to the clubs, Amy," they said.

"You guys don't understand!" she retorted, with tears in her eyes. "I *love* to dance. I'm a vivacious kind of person." But she finally admitted that if she went back to the clubs, she would quickly succumb to drinking and the rest of her previous problems.

The next Sunday, Amy headed for a local church, knowing she needed the reinforcement of strong Christian fellowship. She also called her parents and amazed them with the news of her conversion. The happy report soon spread around the family.

"My brother and sister-in-law called me at least once a week to encourage me. Right before Thanksgiving, he said something very important to me: 'Amy, I just want you to know that if you ever do slip up and make a mistake, don't let the devil hold it over your head. He'll tell you you've blown it, you've ruined your chance at being a Christian. But

God will give you grace. Repent, tell God you're sorry, and go on from there.'"

In fact, she needed that advice all too soon.

For Thanksgiving break, a friend named Dwight invited her to come to Mobile, enjoy his family's soul food, and have a good time. He wasn't an extreme substance abuser, but he did drink.

A friend of his was a bartender, and one night Dwight said, "Amy, let's go by and see my friend real quick, and then we'll go to a movie."

Amy froze with indecision. How should she handle this? She didn't want to offend her host. Finally, she replied, "Well, I don't want to stay long."

"Fine. We'll just have one beer and then leave."

On the way, she told herself, *This is dangerous.* But she couldn't quite say no.

Once inside the bar, she began to physically shake with conviction. Even Dwight noticed it. "Amy, what's wrong?" he asked as they downed the first beer. He offered his coat to keep Amy warm. He even had the bartender turn off the fans.

But the shaking continued.

The next round of beers came, and as Amy drank, she argued with herself. *What am I doing! I'm no better than those kids back at the Christian college who were total hypocrites.*

The drinking had a way of making Amy want to smoke. She asked to borrow a cigarette.

"Hey, I thought you stopped that," Dwight said.

"Yeah, well . . ."

The battle inside Amy raged on. *Okay, I have three options. Either I go back into the "world" and just forget Christianity . . . or I act like a Christian hypocrite . . . or I'm going to get out of this scene and live for God.*

She tells what happened next:

"First I ruled out the middle option. I hate hypocrites!

"Then I got scared thinking about going back into the world. If I did that, it could truly be the end for me, I feared."

"I went to the ladies' room, looked in the mirror—and made up my mind. *I'm not doing this anymore,* I said. When I walked back out, Dwight said we should leave—which was a good thing, because by this time I was half-drunk.

"On the way to Dwight's house, I kept telling myself to hold firm. Once I reached the guest room of his house and closed the door behind me, I got out my Bible and said, 'Okay, God—I'm sorry. I screwed up. I'm not going to do this anymore. Please forgive me for this evening.'"

She awoke the next morning with total peace. While reading her Bible, she remembered what her brother had told her over the phone. God would forgive her and give her another chance. She breathed a prayer of thanks and felt no condemnation.

When she saw Dwight that morning, she said, "I made a big mistake last night."

"Oh, really?" he replied. "No big deal."

"No, I'm serious," she announced. "Never again."

A few days later, during a phone call, her mother said, "Amy, when you come home for Christmas, the pastor here wants you to share your testimony in church."

"No way!" she responded. "I will *not* do that. I can't possibly face those people, after all the stuff they watched me do when I was in high school."

But after several more requests, Amy finally gave in. The day came. She stood in front of her girlhood church—and began crying. She could not say a word for several minutes. As she looked out at the congregation, there were tears all over the building.

Finally she began to speak. It turned out to be a powerful witness of the life-changing power of God.

Some of Amy's high school friends had come to hear her that morning. While some applauded her, others said, "You're in your religious phase now. You'll get over it."

But Amy has never gotten over it. Years have passed since that day, and her walk with God remains solid.

In college Amy had been studying criminal justice with the aim of joining the police force or working for the FBI—another evidence of her personal bent toward "something dangerous." She liked living life on the edge. "That's how I got my excitement," she admits. "But now I felt that God wanted me to switch to youth services so I could work with other young people like myself. He seemed to say, 'You can share with them the love you've found, the difference I've made in your life.'"

Amy finished her degree at Auburn even though she was eager to get into youth ministry right away. Her pastor's wife, among others, encouraged her to stay in school.

Amy stayed solid in her faith in spite of participating in a campus ministry that turned out to be extremist. Instead of carefully guiding her in discipleship, the group instilled a great deal of fear. Amy was assigned prematurely to help "disciple" another girl who was a witch. Strange occult phenomena began happening at Amy's apartment, and she was besieged with horrific nightmares.

Still, she hung tough. She kept crying out to God for relief and strength. In time Amy realized that these were false teachers, so she extricated herself from the group. A year later, she enrolled at Christian Life College in the Chicago suburb of Mount Prospect for a second bachelor's degree, this one in pastoral studies.

There Amy found herself drawn to a young man with a similar vision for helping urban youth. Their friendship deepened. Amy knew, of course, that sooner or later she would have to reveal the details of her past. She dreaded that day.

"Finally I got up the courage to tell him all my history. I was so scared. But God had prepared his heart to hear it.

"The amazing thing to me," she continues, "is that even though he grew up in the city, used to be in a gang, and has messed around with drinking and drugs—he's still a virgin! The dream of my high school days long ago has come true in spite of what I've done. It's like that verse in 2 Timothy 2:13 says—'If we are faithless, he will remain faithful, for he cannot disown himself.'

"God took my confession that day in that little south Alabama church and rewarded me with so much more than I deserve. He is just an incredibly merciful God."

what do

i do with the

memories?

When the blowtorch of exposure has finally turned away, we are left in a feverish state. The perspiration beads of memory stand thick upon our foreheads, adrenaline still speeds through our bloodstream, and we know it will be a long time before normalcy returns.

At such a time, we almost wish for amnesia. If only the past could be erased, if we could dismiss the pictures that flash in living color upon the screens of our minds. Instead, our misdeeds are rerun over and over, as if on a closed-loop film, from the beginning to the awful conclusion and back to the start. We force our brain to switch subjects, but before we know it, there we are again, thinking about it for the thousandth time. We identify with David, who, after his affair, wrote, "My sin is always before me" (Ps. 51:3).

Memory, we realize, is a two-edged sword; though it has served us well in the past, it now turns and threatens to destroy us. Memory is one of God's great gifts, a unique part of our creation as human beings in his image, but for the moment we would just as soon be a bit less gifted.

What do we do with our memories? Several options are available to us.

1. We can become their prisoner. The replay machinery of the brain has a vast power supply, and the tapes do not wear out with use; if anything, they become more indelible. It is thus altogether possible to live for weeks, months, and even years in a vicious trap of the past. What happened was quite possibly the greatest trauma of our lives; we had never been through anything like it before. The ordinary days that preceded it were not nearly so dramatic; we are now mesmerized by our days of infamy.

Emotionally, we ricochet from shame to anger to guilt to fear and back again. It is as if the four walls of the room have mottoes on them, and we carom from one to the next:

"What a fool I was!"

"God must be terribly angry with me."

"I wonder what people are saying now."

"The future is completely shot, isn't it?"

Round and round we go, from one anxiety to another, while the events themselves echo through our heads.

Dr. Haddon Robinson, one of the great preachers of our time, has caught the intensity of this whirlpool in his contrast of two disciples, Peter and Judas. According to Matthew 26:75, Peter "went outside and wept bitterly." A few verses later, we read, "When Judas, who had betrayed him, saw that Jesus was condemned, he was seized with remorse. Then he went away and hanged himself" (Matt. 27:3, 5).

"Two broken men appear side by side on the stage of Scripture," notes Dr. Robinson. "When life overwhelmed one man, it marked his end, but for the other it was a place to begin again. . . . One came to the end of the line and demanded, 'Stop the world; I want off.' The second arrived at the end of the line and requested a transfer.

"For many men and women the agony of Judas and Peter becomes their own. . . . They arrive at a midnight moment. Hope disappears and they reach the end. Like Peter and Judas they face a choice—one that despair always offers—between remorse and repentance, between dying and weeping.

"While both men denied Jesus—in fact, betrayed him— they did so for different reasons. Peter, it appears, denied Jesus because he did not want to die. Judas betrayed Jesus because he would not accept life as it is. He could not believe that for Jesus the path to glory led past a cross. In that sense, Judas was completely consistent. When he could not get life to suit him, he rejected it totally, completely, finally.

"Peter, on the other hand, stumbled through the worst weekend of his life until his risen Lord restored his hope and so changed him that the threat of death lost its power over him. Throughout the following years this same man risked his life to tell his countrymen the gospel of Christ."[1]

A second option, as time goes on, is even more deadly than the first.

2. *We can embellish our memories.* We can play with the dials as the tape moves along, heightening this, intensifying that, warping something else. While we are not likely to make major changes in the story, we can, over a period of time, remember the facts as even worse than they were.

Or, more commonly, we begin to place negative interpretations upon the facts. The reason we did such and such, we conclude, was that we're simply rotten individuals who always make a mess of things. All our vague misgivings and self-doubts link up with these events as proof of our worthlessness.

The next step of embellishment is to put ourselves on trial. Our memories serve as evidence of guilt, after which we act as judge to pass sentence upon ourselves. The married woman who had sex before her wedding night concludes that she must now deny herself any pleasure during physical union as a form of penance. The man who mismanaged his business into bankruptcy decides that he should be a day laborer from now on. Judas goes out to commit suicide.

3. *We can release our memories.* We can allow ourselves, with God's help, to lose track of some things! Although such behavior is not tolerated from computers, it is perfectly all right for humans. Our memory is *supposed* to be selective. The painful things are meant to recede over time, while the good things keep shining bright.

We smile at the widow who, as the months pass following her husband's death, speaks of him in increasingly glowing terms. When he was alive, she often complained and criticized, but now that he's gone, he was a saint.

Well, why not? Her memory is going through a sorting process, keeping the warm and beautiful while it discards the junk.

It is the Enemy who likes to hang on to the rubbish so he can keep using it against us. He enjoys exhuming it before our faces time and again, reminding us of how dreadful we were. He doesn't want us to release those memories, to forget.

In contrast, we see in Scripture the vivid example of the apostle Paul, who had enough nightmares in his past to paralyze him for life. He could close his eyes at any moment and see himself guarding a pile of coats while, a few yards away, the skull of Stephen was being smashed by flying rocks. He could remember a score or more of midnight raids on the homes of Christians . . . beating down doors, jerking men, women, and children out of bed, hauling them off to dungeons. He had terrorized a whole region, from Jerusalem to Damascus, until not a Christian was left who did not wince at the mention of his name.

Yet he rose to a height of apostleship that changed the Mediterranean world. How did he do it? Listen as he tells the Philippian church:

"Not that I ... have already been made perfect, but I press on to take hold of that for which Christ Jesus took hold of me. Brothers, I do not consider myself yet to have taken hold of it. *But one thing I do: Forgetting what is behind* and straining toward what is ahead, I press on toward the goal to win the prize for which God has called me heavenward in Christ Jesus" (3:12–14, italics added).

Can you imagine how that must have thrilled the slave girl in the Philippian congregation who had given herself to demonic fortune-telling in the local marketplace until Paul came to town? Can you imagine its impact on the jailer, sitting a few rows farther back, as he contemplated the inmates he had almost certainly clubbed and maimed in years past? *Forgetting what is behind ... straining toward what is ahead ... press on.*

E. M. Blaiklock, the New Zealand scholar, says that the imagery behind Paul's words is a Roman chariot race, the kind most of us remember from *Ben Hur*:

> The charioteer stood on a tiny platform over sturdy wheels and axle. His knees were pressed against the curved rail, and his thighs flexed. He bent forward at the waist, stretching out hands and head over the horses' backs. This is surely what he [Paul] means by "stretching out to the things before." The reins were wound round the body, and braced on the reins the body formed a taut spring. It can easily be seen how completely the charioteer was at the mercy of his team's sure feet and his own fine driving skill. ... In his intense preoccupation the driver dare not cast a glance at "the things behind." The roaring crowd, crying praise or blame, the racing of his rivals,

all else had perforce to be forgotten. One object only could fill the driver's eye, the point to which he drove at the end of each lap.[2]

It is not our job to be sportswriters, analyzing the race for its flaws, its flukes, its missed opportunities, keeping a historical record. We are *in* the race, not up in the grandstand or the press box, and it is our job to push on to the finish.

What has happened in the past may not, in the end, be as important as *how we choose to feel and think* about what has happened. The way we choose to treat our memories has more to do with the future than the events themselves. If we are consumed with driving toward the goal Christ has held out for us, the past is not all that relevant.

Paul, writing to the seasoned believers at Ephesus (he had spent a full year and a half as their pastor), urged them to abandon the negative thought patterns of those around them, "to put off your old self . . . to be made new in the attitude of your minds; and to put on the new self, created to be like God in true righteousness and holiness" (4:22–24).

We have, in modern times, gotten a bad taste in our mouths at the mention of words such as *holiness*; we immediately think about legalism and long lists of restrictions. We fail to remember that *holy* comes from the same root as *whole, health, heal*, and even *hale* (as in *hale and hearty*). Holiness is not legalism; holiness is healthiness. God intends to make us whole persons by calling us to take on new attitudes, future-oriented attitudes.

This does not happen overnight. The New Birth is not the total cure, but only the initial treatment in the process of bringing us to wholeness. Our return to God after a downfall is not a once-for-all miracle; it is rather a restarting of the change process toward emotional and spiritual health.

The important thing is not to stall at any point along the way, to quit the race. In the next segments of this book, we will probe in more detail how bad memories are released, the role of confession and forgiveness, and the return of equilibrium. In the familiar words of Hebrews 12:1, "Let us throw off everything that hinders . . . let us run with perseverance the race marked out for us."

For Your Reflection

1. Spend some time meditating on Ephesians 4:17–24. Notice especially the many references to mental states, attitudes, perceptions. What are the contrasts between verses 17–19 and 20–24?
2. In Philippians 3, how does Paul show his orientation toward the future? What differences do you think this made in his life and ministry?
3. When are you most plagued with recurring bad memories? What time of the day or week? On what occasions? How can you prepare to deal more firmly with those times of difficulty? If you plan ahead, what could be different next time?

"Fear not."

Genesis 15:1; 21:17; 46:3
Exodus 14:13; 20:20
Numbers 14:9; 21:34
Deuteronomy 1:21; 3:2, 22; 20:3; 31:6, 8
Joshua 8:1; 10:8, 25
Judges 6:23
1 Samuel 12:20; 23:17
1 Kings 17:13
2 Kings 6:16
1 Chronicles 28:20

2 Chronicles 20:17

Isaiah 7:4; 35:4; 41:10, 13–14; 43:1, 5; 44:2, 8; 51:7; 54:4, 14

Jeremiah 30:10; 46:27–28

Lamentations 3:57

Ezekiel 3:9

Daniel 10:12, 19

Joel 2:21

Zechariah 8:13, 15

Matthew 1:20; 10:26, 28, 31; 28:5

Luke 1:13, 30; 2:10; 5:10; 8:50; 12:7, 32

John 12:15

Acts 27:24

Hebrews 13:6

Revelation 1:17; 2:10

I went down to the potter's house, and I saw him working at the wheel. But the pot he was shaping from the clay was marred in his hands; so the potter formed it into another pot, shaping it as seemed best to him.

Then the word of the Lord came to me: "O house of Israel, can I not do with you as this potter does?" declares the LORD. "Like clay in the hand of the potter, so are you in my hand."

—Jeremiah 18:3–6

the fruits
of confession

a time

to speak

"I don't want to talk about it."

We have all used that phrase more than once in our lives, sometimes for better reasons that others. Unpleasant events large and small have been dismissed by it, or at least postponed for later handling. We have felt deep within us that words would only make matters worse, that we couldn't express ourselves accurately anyhow, or that we'd be taken out of context. The best policy, we concluded, was silence.

It is only natural in the wake of a major mistake that we should keep to ourselves for a period. That does not mean that we are at a standstill. Much of the progress outlined thus far—regaining our confidence in the God who rebuilds, meditating upon the Scriptures, facing the facts, dealing with our memories—must be inaudible. Nonetheless, we are a long way from where we started.

But perhaps there is a significance in the sequence of the immortal words in Ecclesiastes, "A time to be silent and a time to speak" (3:7). The Bible seems to indicate that after our initial stages of privacy, we must come to *verbalize* some things:

- The facts that we have already acknowledged in our heads
- God's view of those facts
- Our sorrow for what we have done
- Our desire to be forgiven and walk a different road in the future

Those words are what we call *confession*: the acknowledging in actual language of how things are.

If we are going to open our mouths at all on the subject, we had better start with talking to God. He is, after all, the one listener who will get it straight and not misinterpret us.

Listen to the prophet's call:

> Take words with you
>   and return to the LORD.
> Say to him:
>   "Forgive all our sins
> and receive us graciously,
>   that we may offer the fruit of our lips.
> Assyria cannot save us;
>   we will not mount war-horses.
> We will never again say 'Our gods'
>   to what our own hands have made,
>   for in you the fatherless find compassion."
>
> Hosea 14:4–5

The call to confession rings throughout the Bible, from the patriarchs to the prophets to John the Baptist to the familiar words of 1 John 1:9 near the end—"If we confess our sins, he is faithful and just and will forgive us our sins and purify us from all unrighteousness." God knows we must do more than think about it; we must *say it* to him, in order that the issues of guilt and pardon can be clarified.

But what if we would "rather not"? Can we not just keep moving along toward restoration and wholeness without this embarrassment? The Thirty-second Psalm explains what happens if we try:

> *When I kept silent,*
>   *my bones wasted away*
>   *through my groaning all day long.*
> *For day and night*
>   *your hand was heavy upon me;*
> *my strength was sapped*
>   *as in the heat of summer.*
> *Then I acknowledged my sin to you*
>   *and did not cover up my iniquity.*
> *I said, "I will confess*
>   *my transgressions to the LORD"—*
> *and you forgave*
>   *the guilt of my sin.*
>
> *Therefore let everyone who is godly pray to you*
>   *while you may be found. . . .*
> *Do not be like the horse or the mule,*
>   *which have no understanding.*
>
>   Psalm 32:3–6, 9

There is no escaping the fact that confession implies a willingness to die. It is painful; it means giving up the old masquerade of okay-ness. It means admitting not only to ourselves but also to a perfect God that we have blown it.

But let us not forget that on the far side of dying is resurrection. Confession is but a way station through which we pass en route to new life and health.

And in order for God to bring us to that destination, he sometimes requires us to repair the relationships we have damaged with other people. We must talk not only to God in heaven; we must summon the courage and humility to talk to certain individuals here on earth. If, for example, our husband or wife is to be a part of God's bright future for us, we cannot enter that future without dealing with the hurts we may have inflicted. Confession is not only vertical; it is horizontal.

We shrink from such honesty for the same reasons that we hesitated to come to God—and for some other reasons as well. We don't know whether our confession will be accepted or turned down; we fear an attack of blame instead of a welcoming spirit. In some cases we rationalize, "What they don't know won't hurt them," refusing all the while to admit that what they don't know is killing *us*, festering inside, poisoning all attempts at sincere dialogue. The days and weeks pass along in a haze of playacting; only a brave act of confession will clear the air.

When the prodigal son in Jesus' story thought about going home, he knew he would need to do more than just walk through the front door. *He would have to say something.* He planned his sentences even while in the pigpen: "I will set out and go back to my father and say to him: Father, I have sinned against heaven and against you. I am no longer worthy to be called your son; make me like one of your hired men" (Luke 15:18–19).

As it turned out, he got only partway through his speech before his ecstatic father cut him off with the order for the best robe, the ring, and the fattened calf. Nevertheless, the words were important. They crystallized, for the son most of all, the dramatic turnaround in his life. It is often the same with us. God and the people we have offended need to hear us say it— but more than they, we need to hear ourselves say it. It is then a matter of record, a fact of a certain day, time, and location that we can recall for the rest of our lives.

One person, after an excruciating public acknowledgment of his fall, looked back and said, "If there had been no confession, there would have been no chance for the people of God to respond to me. They would simply have had to wait in silence, wondering. But as soon as I spoke—hard as it was to do—it released them to reach out in love and forgiveness. The healing process could begin."

In response to our definitive statements, God makes a few proclamations of his own. The Scriptures are full of his promises to forgive completely, utterly, irrevocably. While some people may struggle with whether to write off the past, God does not. He forgives totally; if he didn't, he wouldn't be God.

Fallen Christians are sometimes not sure about this. Can God really forgive as completely now as when we first came to him for salvation? Doesn't he keep some sort of blacklist?

"I will forgive their wickedness," God announced through Jeremiah after about a thousand years of Israel's ups and downs, "and will remember their sins no more" (31:34).

David claimed in Psalm 103:12 that our transgressions are removed "as far as the east is from the west." Anyone who has ever flown from New York to New Delhi, or from Tokyo to Tel Aviv, can appreciate that.

Ephesians 1:7–8 explains why God grants such a clean slate. Our forgiveness, technically, is not ours; it is Christ's! "*In him* we have redemption through his blood, the forgiveness of sins, in accordance with the riches of God's grace that he lavished on us with all wisdom and understanding" (italics added).

What does it mean to be "in Christ"? This common New Testament expression is well illustrated by Bruce Narramore and Bill Counts in their book, *Freedom from Guilt*:

> Suppose you put a piece of paper between the pages of a book, then close the book. Whatever happens to the book happens to the paper. If you throw the book away, you throw the paper away. If you put the book in a safe

place, you safeguard the paper. If the paper is dirty and spotted, you don't see the dirt at all—you only see the book. The same is true of our position in Christ. When God looks on us, He sees us "in Christ." He doesn't see our dirt. He sees us just as clean and pure as Jesus Christ himself.[1]

Do we *feel* forgiven and restored after confession to God? It doesn't matter. The fact is, we are. We are in Christ, and that is enough.

Gwynn Lewis, a young Ohioan who ruined his life with drugs and eventually set up a drug dealing operation in Ecuador, was finally arrested along with his live-in girlfriend. He spent months rotting in a rat-infested prison, until a missionary began to visit him and eventually led him to faith in Christ. The missionary also helped get him released and back to the United States. On the next-to-last page of his short book, *Nightmare in Paradise*, Lewis says:

> People sometimes ask me if I feel any guilt or remorse for my former life. The answer to that is *absolutely not*! I have been forgiven; I *feel* forgiven totally and completely. I am a new person. Part of that feeling is due to Jerry Reed, I'm sure. He treated me like a new man even before I was. Never once did he hold back; the love and respect I felt from him were genuine, and better than I probably deserved. From him I learned something of God's grace, and that goes a long way toward erasing any guilt that might have lingered.[2]

The full sweep of repentance and restoration can be seen in the second chapter of Joel's prophecy in the Old Testament—a beautiful outline of God's plan for tripped-up people. The nation has fallen into serious sin, but here, in what might be called the Bible's Comeback Chapter, are four important events:

1. The Punishment (vv. 1–11). Sin and backsliding bring, in this case, an invasion of locusts that strip the countryside of everything green.

> *they leap over the mountaintops,*
> *like a crackling fire consuming stubble,*
>   *like a mighty army drawn up for battle. . . .*
> *They climb into the houses;*
>   *like thieves they enter through the windows. . . .*
> *It is dreadful.*
> *Who can endure it?*
>
>   Joel 2:5, 9, 11

The point is clear: Sin has consequence. We do not get away with things that displease God. But then—

2. The Repentance (vv. 12–17). People who have been devastated have an option after all. They do not have to simply go on suffering.

> *"Even now," declares the LORD,*
>   *"return to me with all your heart,*
>   *with fasting and weeping and mourning."*
> *Rend your heart*
>   *and not your garments.*
> *Return to the LORD your God,*
>   *for he is gracious and compassionate,*
> *slow to anger and abounding in love,*
>   *and he relents from sending calamity.*
> *Who knows but that he may turn and have pity*
>   *and leave behind a blessing—*
>
>   Joel 2:12–14

And what will be the result of this confession? Will it do any good?

3. The Restoration (vv. 18–27). The passage begins with the pivotal word "Then" and proceeds to tell all that God will do. The "northern army" will be pushed out; the land will again produce crops; rainfall will return; the threshing floors will be filled. And then comes an almost incredible bonus, far beyond what we deserve:

> *"I will repay you for the years the locusts have eaten—*
> *the great locust and the young locust,*
> *the other locusts and the locust swarm—*
> *my great army that I sent among you.*
> *You will have plenty to eat, until you are full,*
> *and you will praise the name of the LORD your God*
> *who has worked wonders for you;*
> *never again will my people be shamed."*

Joel 2:25–26

It would be enough to gain relief from the pressures we brought upon ourselves. But to be repaid for lost time is almost unfathomable.

The Comeback Chapter concludes with a glimpse of . . .

4. The New Usefulness (vv. 28–32).

> *"And afterward,*
> *I will pour out my Spirit on all people.*
> *Your sons and daughters will prophesy,*
> *your old men will dream dreams,*
> *your young men will see visions. . . .*
> *There will be deliverance,*
> *as the LORD has said,*
> *among the survivors*
> *whom the LORD calls."*

Joel 2:28, 32

This prophecy was fulfilled specifically on the Day of Pentecost, but as Peter explained to the curious crowd that day, "The promise is for you and your children and for all who are far off—for all whom the Lord our God will call" (Acts 2:39). We must not limit the words of Joel to one event of history; God is still in the business of pouring out his Spirit on repentant people, causing those who have wrecked their dreams to dream new ones, showing wonders not only in the heavens but also on the earth—in the lives of "the survivors."

But in our eager yearning for stages 3 and 4, we cannot by-pass stage 2. The "Then" of Joel 2:18 and 27 must necessarily follow the "Even now" of verse 12. The fireworks of verses 28–32 begin with "And afterward. . . ." Confession and repentance are the keys that unlock the door to God's favor, and there are apparently no side entrances.

For Your Reflection

1. Study the Comeback Chapter (Joel 2) for yourself, marking the four sections in the margins of your Bible, and noting the progression from one to the next.
2. Do you tense up at the thought of actually blurting out your confession to God? Use Daniel 9:4–19 as a model for praying. Notice how honest Daniel is, how willing to "put all the cards on the table." After you've read the passage, take a sheet of paper and write your own paraphrase, based on your own personal situation. (Daniel's forthrightness, by the way, resulted in a visit from no less than the angel Gabriel—see the rest of the chapter.)
3. If you're still not sure whether God forgives and restores adulterers, robbers, cheats, and other scoundrels, see Ezekiel 18:10–13, 21–23, 27–28.
4. Begin praying for the inner strength to clear the air with the people you've wronged. Then follow through; do your part to answer your own prayer.

Dr. Richard D. Dobbins, a veteran of more than twenty-five years in the pastorate, now heads an Akron-based counseling and mental health ministry. He travels widely to speak on how personal wholeness can be gained through spiritual avenues. On one of his cassettes entitled "The Healing of Memories," he tells the following story of a woman he refers to as "Evelyn."

She grew up in an Assembly of God church; her father was a board member. During her teen years she dated the president of the youth group, and they prematurely committed themselves to each other. She became pregnant.

At six months in her pregnancy, the people of that church put pressure on the pastor to dismiss her father from the board. They also moved to force her and the youth president to stand up on Sunday morning and confess that they had done something wrong.

We hurt when we hear things like that, don't we? And yet these things were done in the name of keeping the church clean.

Needless to say, the wounds were deep and raw and ugly and open. Miracle of miracles, both of them stayed in the church. It wasn't easy, but they lived it down. . . .

Now, at forty-some years of age, she was sitting in my office. In the first two sessions, she commented, "There's something I need to talk to you about—but I'm afraid if you know, you'll never have any respect for me."

What I didn't know then was that one of the teenagers in the church who had been her friend when all of this happened, who knew all of the sordid details, had moved away—and now, after twenty-some years, was moving back.

And in Evelyn's mind, *time stood still.* She and her friend were teenagers again, and she was threatened with great fear that this woman was coming back to begin the story all over.

In our third session together, Evelyn told me her past. She had never really dealt with it before. It had been there, like a raw abrasive in her marriage. She couldn't have right feelings toward her husband, because she wasn't sure whether he had married her because he loved her or because he had to. He had told her a hundred times or more that he had married her because of love. But the emotional blockage just would not let the message come through.

I will never forget the day when she began to weep convulsively in my office, and I said to her, "Evelyn . . . have you asked the Lord to forgive you of this?"

"Ho!" she said. "Have I asked the Lord to forgive me? I've asked him a hundred times!"

"Well . . . do you believe he has?"

"Oh, yes, I believe the Lord has forgiven me—but how can I forgive myself?"

And then I said quietly and slowly, "Oh . . . are you holier than God is?" I paused. "Must God sacrifice *another* Son just for the sake of your conscience?" Another pause. "If the death of Christ was good enough for God, isn't it good enough for you?"

It is hard for me to describe the beautiful scene that transpired as the Holy Spirit pressed that truth to her heart. She broke down and wept for ten minutes or more. The expression on her countenance when she finished weeping was obviously changed. After we prayed to end our session that day, she said, "This is the first time in over twenty years that I feel no condemnation."

Jesus died that the people of God might never suffer from guilt or fear. "If we confess our sins, he is faithful and just to forgive us our sins, and to cleanse us from *all* unrighteousness."

fRee

INDeeD

When we speak of confession and forgiveness, we often worry about two extremes: making it all too easy, and making it all too hard. On the one hand, is it really so simple as a mere "I'm sorry"? Surely we must agonize more than that. But on the other hand, would all of our agonizing turn the trick in the end? King Henry IV of Germany was once kept waiting barefoot in the Alpine snow for three January days before the pope would forgive him. Was that really necessary? Does not Jesus invite us to come simply and accept the atonement he won on the cross?

Dr. Richard Dobbins, the pastor-psychologist mentioned earlier, has built a helpful model of the dynamics at work in processing guilt or regret.[1] He grew up in a wing of Protestantism that urged people carrying spiritual burdens to do what was rather quaintly called "praying through." By that the old-timers meant more than just talking to God with head bowed;

they meant staying at the altar of the church and working through the issues in prayer until a sense of release finally came. It might take an hour or longer; it might even require several sessions. But in the end, the time was well spent.

Dobbins suggests that "praying through" was more than just a quirk of Bible Belt revivalism. His clients now use it, in fact, as a form of self-help between counseling sessions. The process has four steps:

1. *Name the damage intellectually.* Tell God what actually happened. Identify the source of the current pain.

As has already been discussed, this is sometimes hard to do. We don't want to be this honest. But in the presence of a Father who loves us and has promised not to evict us, we are safe.

2. *Allow our feelings about what has happened to come to the surface and flush out.* We may have repressed our anger, self-hatred, or disappointment for a long time, but we can only get rid of such emotions by emptying them. Our destructive thought patterns will never change until we express them, preferably alone to God. If this is accompanied by crying or other kinds of outbursts, we need not be embarrassed. The emotional reality is as serious as the objective reality.

At the end of this phase, we have a sense of great relief. This is the time "when the burden lifts," as some have called it.

But we are not finished. We need more than just a ventilation of tension.

3. *Meditate; let the Word and the Holy Spirit show how our old perceptions have been hurting us, and wait for a new meaning or interpretation of the facts.* As Hebrews 4:12 says, "The word of God is living and active. Sharper than any double-edged sword, it penetrates even to dividing soul and spirit, joints and marrow; it judges the thoughts and attitudes of the heart." If we are willing to spend portions of our prayer time listening rather than talking, we will find God shedding new light on our

circumstance. He will move us past our mistake; we will hear ourselves saying, "At least now I know some of the worst things about myself. I can't be fooled that way again!"

And as we wait in God's presence, we become aware of options for our future. We are released from our first fixation on the tragedy; we find less painful ways of thinking about our lives.

4. Replace the old, hurtful interpretations with the new ones gained through meditation and prayer. We can lay aside the thoughts that have been jabbing at us as we take up the divine perspectives. We can even begin to praise God for the relief he has granted and the new meaning he has given to the event.

"Writing down the new way of looking at the old hurt often helps to fix it in your mind," says Dobbins. "If you even add the date of your experience of relief, you can then remind yourself when tempted to pick up the old hurt again."

An example: Imagine a woman whose pregnancy was unintended. She is now suffering from post-natal depression. The fact of the baby's presence is clear enough (step one). In step two, she may go ahead and articulate her anger at herself and/or her husband for not using proper birth control methods. She may also say that she feels terribly wicked for resenting this beautiful, innocent child. She admits to the Lord that she is, so far, a begrudging parent.

But as she meditates, some new ideas come to the surface. Her career plans are not dashed forever. She can resume her work outside the home in a few years. Things are perhaps not as bad as she first thought. She eventually takes up mothering as a valid and rewarding part of her life.

Several writers and teachers in the area of inner healing have outlined similar steps to "praying through." They lead hurting people through an imaginary replay of past traumas—only this time, the person visualizes Jesus in each scene, healing, soothing, binding up wounds, placing new interpretations on all that happened.

Narramore and Counts explain the benefits of what they term "constructive sorrow"—something sharply different from "psychological guilt," or self-condemnation. The contrast is clear in Paul's comments to the Corinthian church:

> Even if I caused you sorrow by my letter, I do not regret it.... For you became sorrowful as God intended and so were not harmed in any way by us. Godly sorrow brings repentance that leads to salvation and leaves no regret, but worldly sorrow brings death.
>
> 2 Corinthians 7:8–10

The difference, say the co-authors, is that "psychological guilt produces self-inflicted misery. Constructive sorrow produces a positive change of behavior."[2]

> David's full confession, recorded in Psalm 51, reflects both psychological guilt and constructive sorrow. If David had immediately repented over his sins, he would have avoided much psychological guilt. But the long delay, compounded by further deception, loneliness, and David's own psychological makeup programmed him for destructive guilt....
>
> Psychological guilt helped keep David in spiritual paralysis for a year! Constructive sorrow brought him immediate repentance and release.[3]

Call it whatever you like—the process of confession and forgiveness is a strategic part of starting again. And experience has shown *we usually need more than one time through the process* before we are fully restored. Dobbins notes that people sometimes need to recycle even fifteen or twenty times as they gradually lay to rest various segments of their inner pain. "The trouble is, many Christians get through praying before they've 'prayed through,'" he quips. "We have all seen the plaques that read, 'Prayer changes things.' It's my observation that prayer usually changes people, and people change things."

In an age that calls for instant fixes, we are not always patient with such a gradual approach. We would do well to heed the oriental proverb, "Don't push the river." The stream of God's grace will carry us where we need to go; our thrashing about will only exhaust us. When we find ourselves like Joseph in a pit of calamity, we too often pray for a helicopter evacuation rather than wait to be made ruler of all Egypt in time.

Our task is rather to cooperate with the process, to continue confessing our wrongs and our destructive attitudes as we become aware of them, and to receive the Holy Spirit's new interpretations in return. Hebrews 12 exhorts us not to resist God's disciplining work; it is a sign that he takes us seriously. "No discipline seems pleasant at the time, but painful. Later on, however, it produces a harvest of righteousness and peace for those who have been trained by it" (v.11).

How will we know that we are whole again? Some signs that the process is reaching completion are:

- *When we can thank God for the lessons learned through the ordeal.* Our new insights have shown us that we are better, wiser Christians now, and we are grateful.
- *When we can talk about what happened without getting upset.* When the subject comes up, either in general or specifics, we can handle it. We no longer turn red, hold our breath, or leave the room. When the pastor mentions the name of "our" sin or shortcoming from the pulpit, we don't flinch. We have been thoroughly forgiven.
- *When we can revisit the scene or the people involved without getting upset.* Granted, it may not always be wise to go back to a certain town or ring a certain doorbell, for the shock that other people might experience. But for ourselves, we have the capacity to do so without

falling to pieces. God has swept the shame and guilt out of our consciousness, and we are free indeed.

The way of confession and forgiveness is neither too easy nor too hard. It brings us to terms with God, and it sets us in the end on a new and promising course. It releases us to enter a future of brightness and hope.

For Your Reflection

Engage in several episodes of "praying through," using the four steps outlined in this chapter. Use the following Scriptures for meditation, or others to which the Holy Spirit directs you.

- Psalm 51
- Jeremiah 31
- James 1

In his book Let Us Enjoy Forgiveness, *Judson Cornwall explains and then illustrates how completely God removes our sins once they are confessed. This excerpt begins with a comment on Colossians 2:13–14, "He forgave us all our sins, having canceled the written code, with its regulations, that was against us and that stood opposed to us; he took it away, nailing it to his cross."*

The more common Greek word for the cancellation of a contract is *chiazein*, which means to write the Greek letter *chi*, which is the same shape as a capital X, right across the document. This was called a "cross out." But Paul uses the Greek word *exaleiphein*, which literally means "to wash over," as in whitewashing, or "to wipe out." The ink used in Paul's day was basically soot mixed with gum and diluted with water. It would last for a long time and retain its color, but a wet sponge passed over the surface of the papyrus could wash the paper as clean as it had been before the writing had been inscribed on it. This is the word Paul uses here. Our sins have not merely been canceled out; they have been blotted out. . . .

God made this truth tremendously clear to me when I was pastoring on the West Coast. I had been burdened for a pastor who had been defrocked by his denomination for immorality and had moved to my community to start life over as a watchman for a plywood mill. Over a period of many months, we lunched together and came to know each other quite well. I continuously sought to cause him to accept the forgiveness he used to preach and encouraged him to live as a forgiven man, but it was difficult for him, since he had lived most of his life in the concept that God has a separate standard for ministers. After more than a year, the reality of God's forgiveness began to dawn upon him. He and his wife attended our church, and he occasionally ministered for me. It was great to see this guilt-ridden brother begin to accept the fullness of God's glorious forgiveness. In time, his denomination recognized the change in him and reinstated him, offering him a small church to begin his ministry anew.

The day he was to leave to accept this new charge, I phoned him on his job to assure him of my continued interest and prayers, only to be informed that he had changed his mind.

"Why?" I inquired. "I thought it was all settled."

"Judson," he said, "I just can't go through with it. After what I did in my last church, I don't deserve another chance. I'm not worthy to preach the Gospel of Christ anymore."

Shocked and disgusted, I hung up on him and went directly to the prayer room in the church.

"Lord," I prayed, "have I been mistaken about him all along? Did he really confess his sin, or did he merely admit his guilt? Is he caught up in self-condemnation, or is he still guilty in your sight?"

God's answer came in the form of an immediate vision. With my eyes still closed in prayer, I saw myself in a large room that had bookcases on all four walls with volumes of leather-bound books from floor to ceiling. It reminded me of a legal library. As I looked at the books, I saw that they were alphabetized by names of people. A large hand with an extended index finger began to move across the books, until it came to the one with this minister's name on it. The book was removed from the shelf, placed on a small table, and opened in such a way that I could see and read the pages. The first page told the story of his birth, and subsequent pages told of his early childhood, of his call into the ministry while he was still in his teens, of his first ministry and pastorate, of his courtship and marriage, and of his climb to a respected position in his denomination. I could only wish I possessed the ability to read as rapidly in real life as I was able to read in that vision. Everything that I read fit what I had come to know about this man.

The top of each page was dated, very much like a diary, and as the pages got closer and closer to the first incidence of adultery, I wondered how God would have it recorded. But when the book opened to that date, the page was absolutely blank, as were succeeding pages for what would be chapters of space. Then when we came to the date of his repentance, it was fully recorded with a marginal gloss that this had produced great rejoicing in heaven. Following this, the pages recorded his progress back into faith, his ministry in our church, his reacceptance into the denomination, and his call to the new church. Puzzled by the many blank pages, I asked if I could have a closer look at them. My request was granted, and I saw that there had been writing on the pages, but that it had been erased. On the bottom of each erased page, in red, were the initials "JC."

True to his word, Jesus Christ had "blotted out the charges proved against you, the list of his commandments which you had not obeyed" (Colossians 2:14 LB). Heaven had no record of this man's sin. The only existing record was in his memory.

Excited with this revelation, I rushed to the phone and called the brother. After I told him what God had shown me, he quit his job, took the church, and re-entered the ministry as a forgiven man.

God does not forgive and then file it away for future reference; he forgives and then erases the record. The pages of transcript that record our sinning are erased clean. Even the tape recording of our confession is erased, so that none will ever have access to our past. The guilt is removed and so is the evidence. This is the way God forgives the repentant one. Acts 3:19 urges us, "Repent ye therefore, and be converted, that your sins may be blotted out [Greek *exaleiphein*], when the times of refreshing shall come from the presence of the Lord" (KJV).

PART FOUR

MOVING ON

IT'S ONLY

HALFTIME

On New Year's Day, 1929, Georgia Tech played University of California in the Rose Bowl. Shortly before halftime, a man named Roy Riegels recovered a fumble for California. Somehow he became confused and started running—sixty-five yards in the wrong direction. One of his teammates, Benny Lom, outdistanced him and downed him just before he would have scored for the opposing team. When California attempted to punt, Tech blocked the kick and scored a safety.

The men filed off the field and went into the dressing room. They sat down on the benches and on the floor, all but Riegels. He put his blanket around his shoulders, sat down in a corner, put his face in his hands, and cried like a baby.

If you have played football, you know that a coach usually has a great deal to say to his team during halftime. That day Coach Nibbs Price was quiet. No doubt he was trying to decide what to do with Riegels.

The timekeeper came in and announced that there were three minutes before playing time. Coach Price looked at the team and said simply, "Men, the same team that played the first half will start the second."

The players got up and started out, all but Riegels. He did not budge. The coach looked back and called to him again; still he didn't move.

Coach Price went over to where Riegels sat and said, "Roy, didn't you hear me? The same team that played the first half will start the second."

Roy Riegels looked up, and his cheeks were wet with a strong man's tears. "Coach," he said, "I can't do it. I've ruined you; I've ruined the University of California; I've ruined myself. I couldn't face that crowd in the stadium to save my life."

Coach Price reached out and put his hand on Riegels's shoulder and said to him, "Roy, get up and go on back; the game is only half over."

Roy Riegels went back, and those Tech men will tell you that they have never seen a man play football as Roy Riegels played that second half. . . .

We take the ball and run in the wrong direction; we stumble and fall and are so ashamed of ourselves that we never want to try again, and He comes to us and bends over us in the person of His Son and says, "Get up and go on back; the game is only half over."

—Haddon W. Robinson

new
things

To be forgiven, to have our blot erased and forgotten, is a great gift.

But to watch God fill the empty space, writing a new thing upon the tablet of our lives, is even greater.

It is the final evidence that he does not hold a grudge, that he has not schemed some kind of residual punishment for us. His love is so complete that it does not stop until he has assured us that we are more than just tolerable in his sight; we are valuable.

Why do we remember Abraham as such a notable man? Because of what God did with him *after* he bolted away from God's plan for his life. He had followed the call to migrate to Canaan, but almost immediately he left. "Now there was a famine in the land, and Abram went down to Egypt to live there for a while because the famine was severe" (Gen. 12:10).

In Egypt, one problem followed another. He began to fear for the safety of his attractive wife. So he plotted with her to lie about their relationship. Sarai was indeed taken into the royal harem for a time. Finally the Lord had to intervene with a plague, which exposed the facts and got Abram expelled from the country with all his caravan.

And that was not all. Somewhere in the process they picked up an Egyptian domestic named Hagar, who proved to be the source of later contention that almost split the marriage. The world today, in fact, has still not recovered from the results of that fiasco, as the descendants of Isaac and Ishmael continue to assail each other in the Middle East.

Abram stumbled back to the Promised Land. Had God written him off now? Would he ever reach his potential? The answer came in Genesis 13:14–17, when the Lord gave him a message of tremendous import: "Lift up your eyes from where you are. . . ." *Don't let the experience in Egypt paralyze you, Abram; get your sights up off the ground.* "And look north and south, east and west. All the land that you see I will give to you and your offspring forever. I will make your offspring like the dust of the earth, so that if anyone could count the dust, then your offspring could be counted. Go, walk through the length and breadth of the land, for I am giving it to you."

Abram is finally on his way to greatness! God's plan has been delayed, but not canceled. There will be a Hebrew nation after all.

Another spectacular example is Jonah, whose preaching brought an entire capital of the ancient world to its knees. Who would have dreamed that Jonah, the man who did his best to torpedo God's will for his life, would end up being the one smashing success among the Old Testament prophets? Taken as a group, they mostly failed. Jeremiah was consistently mocked or else ignored; Amos was thrown out of the king's court; Ezekiel was told in the very beginning that nobody would listen to him. Even Isaiah and Daniel managed only tentative responses from the monarchs they addressed.

But "the Ninevites believed God. They declared a fast, and all of them, from the greatest to the least, put on sackcloth" (Jonah 3:5). The lives of perhaps a half million people were spared as a result.

Why did the pagan Assyrians listen and respond so whole-heartedly to this man? It is tantalizing to wonder whether Jonah told them about his voyage; some have suggested that even his skin and hair might have been bleached by the acids of the fish's stomach, lending credence to his story. After all, Jesus did comment that "Jonah was a sign to the Ninevites" (Luke 11:29).

If so, the event shows us God's amazing power to turn human perversity upside down and use it for good. Even if Jonah did not relate his past on the streets of Nineveh, the results of his ministry force us to admit that mistakes can be overridden.

Had modern Christians been given the chance to coun-sel Jonah between chapters 2 and 3 of his book, after his return from the sea but before going to Nineveh, some of us would almost certainly have said, "Well, yes, my friend, God will forgive you for trying to run away from him, but the future is likely to be second-best from here on. You see, you've missed God's perfect will for your life, and now you must be content with whatever can be salvaged."

In so doing, we betray an overly rigid view of God's plan-ning. We assume he has only one track for each of his children, and all other routes are sure to be bumpy detours. They may get you to heaven in the end, but you'll be exhausted if and when you arrive. You didn't stay in "the perfect will of God."

Such thinking confuses God's foreknowledge with his pre-destining. While he is omniscient and therefore knows all things before they happen (we will never surprise him by our actions), the Scriptures do not tell us that he has narrowed every life choice for every person down to one best option, and any other will cause the universe to wobble.

Erwin W. Lutzer reminds us in his book *Failure: The Back Door to Success* that God's perfect plan for the world got ruined a long time ago—in Eden. Thus, he concludes:

> To talk about the "ideal" life is quite futile. Since we were all born as children of wrath, we have all experienced sins and failures. The only ideal life will be in heaven, and if you are reading this, you're not there!
>
> Of course, within the context of our sinful human condition, God undoubtedly has a plan for everyone's life. . . . But all such plans are made by taking our sinful condition into account. For God, there are no contingencies; He knows the end from the beginning.
>
> What if we should err on one point or another? What if we disobey God and sin greatly? Or marry the "wrong" one? God will not be caught off guard. He will not be forced to activate emergency equipment. *He is prepared to help us in our sin as He was to help Adam in his!*[1]

If God is not only the Creator but also the Creative Manager of the world, he must show at least as much creativity as human managers do. The genius of any business leader lies in shifting and adjusting to a constantly changing economic picture. If what has worked well in the past is starting to falter, he quickly takes note, figures out why, and revises his strategy. If one approach is blocked, he moves on to the second or third. He sees various ways to reach his goals.

Surely God is even smarter at managing people than we are.

One business seminar leader asks his audiences to imagine a railroad track going over a steep mountain. He draws a quick sketch on his chalkboard and then adds, "Now imagine that a train is starting up this side of the mountain while at the same time another train is starting up the other side. And there are no sidings along the way.

"What is needed in this situation?"

The answer, of course, is someone to intervene—someone to look down, as it were, from a spotter plane and see both trains at the same time heading for a collision. He can then take steps to prevent tragedy.

"Such a person has what I call *super-vision*; he is in a position to take in all the factors at once. That's what you men and women must do on your jobs; that's why you're called *supervisors*. You are to see what other people can't or don't see and then take action."

The Ultimate Supervisor, of course, is he who dwells in the heavens. He can see exactly what we are doing with our lives, and he has a vast array of options at his fingertips.

> One day some ink was accidentally spilled onto a beautiful and expensive handkerchief. The mess was observed by an artist who decided to make the best of the situation. So he drew a picture on the cloth and used the blotch of ink as part of the scenery. God is well-equipped to do that for us, if we are prepared to let Him.[2]

The one nagging difficulty, as was mentioned earlier, comes when *other people* are not prepared to let him redeem the blotch. Some are afraid to welcome or encourage the fallen but forgiven Christian for fear of "setting a bad example." They do not want to seem soft on sin, and so they continue in aloofness. Others are downright vindictive; they are determined to serve as God's warden, not accepting the fact that the Judge has already granted pardon.

God does not force such people to change their minds, of course, and their resistance becomes a limitation on what he can do. Though he might want to restore his child to a place of service in the church, the members may steadfastly refuse to allow it. Such is indeed a tragedy.

But our God has not used up his options. Rebuffed at one point, he will simply turn to another. He cares too much to give in to the biases of individuals. The Christ who holds "the power of an indestructible life" (Heb. 7:16) will not be thwarted in the end.

A number of years ago I was speaking at a church in Manitowoc, Wisconsin, a port city on Lake Michigan. My host took me that afternoon to see the harbor area. A lake freighter nearly a block long was tied up, and I stared at the gaping hole in its side that ran from bow to stern, several feet wide.

"What's happening?" I asked. "Why is there such a huge cut all along the ship?"

"They've brought her in here to overhaul her—actually to enlarge her capacity" was the reply. "They have literally sliced the thing right through the middle, jacked up the top half, and now they're welding in pieces to fill the space. When they're done, the ship will carry almost twice as much cargo as before."

I could not help thinking that sometimes human beings get ripped apart as well, and though for a time their lives are an ugly sight to behold, they become bigger people in the end. The painful surgery has enlarged their capacity to serve. God has once again shown his creative management skills, and for that we can only give him praise.

For Your Reflection

1. Can you think of any reasons why God would *not* want to restore and use us after we confess our wrong? Make a list if you can.
2. Read slowly through Psalms 30 and 103, noting all the things God does for us when we turn to him.
3. What pieces of God's new things for you are already taking shape?

Justice: We get what we deserve.
Mercy: We do not get what we deserve.
Grace: We get what we do not deserve.

—Sam Wilson

the making

of a conqueror

How? When? Where?

How will God go about bringing springtime into my life?
How long will it take?

What will happen first? Second? Third?

Will it happen here in the old situation, or somewhere else?

Once our hopes have been raised and our eyes have caught the possibilities, we are suddenly full of questions. We want to know as many details as we can; our impatience mounts as we peer into the still-hazy future for shapes of things to come.

There are no set answers, as the various profiles of individuals in this book illustrate. God's restoration plan for one person is not his plan for another. Sometimes he moves dramatically, quickly, almost catapulting the person into a place he or she could hardly have dreamed of. Sometimes God waits—seeming to do nothing—until finally he makes his move. Many times his renaissance comes in stages, gradually, a little crack of light at first, then a larger beam, until eventually we are out into full sunshine. He has his reasons, and he is hardly obliged to explain them all to us.

But we can imagine at least some of them. If we find our restoration coming a piccc at a time, it could be because:

- He knows *we* need a gradual reentry. We are still learning to depend upon him, and a full-blown responsibility is more than we could handle. We are still in the business of understanding grace and forgiveness, of putting names to what we have just experienced, and believing that it is really true. We have only limited energy for reaching out to help others.

- He is limited by the wariness of other people. Some are not sure whether to get close to us, for fear of "contamination." Just as we are busy sorting things out in our heads, so are they. In the meantime, our opportunities may be confined.

We must resist any tinge of bitterness toward such people; after all, they are as imperfect as we are. It is true that they shouldn't be so slow to accept us; but it is also true that we shouldn't have gotten ourselves into this pocket in the first place. We are in no position to throw stones.

We must also resist any bitterness toward God for his gradual approach. *We must not despise the early stages.* If we are only a choir member in the church now, whereas we headed up a department before; if our mistake has forced us into a different job at less pay; if family relatives are only half as warm toward us now as they were previously; if our friends invite us to be with them only occasionally—we must not give up. We must not assume we have been cursed.

Instead, we must remain steady and give thanks for the progress thus far. It is interesting to note that while 1 Thessalonians 5:18 does not say, "Give thanks *for* all circumstances," it does say, "Give thanks *in* all circumstances." We are not required to put a happy face on everything that happens or to insist that our disappointment is really exhilaration. We do not have to play games with the facts. But we can give thanks in the midst of uncertainty because of our confidence in God. He is bringing us back; he knows what he is doing; and the present is but a stage to something greater.

This gives us a touch of independence. We do not have to be so consumed with such questions as:

- How long must I "wear sackcloth" and act penitent? Am I allowed to smile in public?
- What do I do with *other people's* memories of what I've done?
- How many times must I share my inner feelings with friends, would-be counselors, et al?

These take on a different light when we keep the perspective of God as our ultimate guide and mentor. Paul once commented about a troubled Christian: "To his own master he stands or falls. And he will stand" [Note the confidence!], "for the Lord is able to make him stand" (Rom. 14:4).

We will stand much faster, of course, if the local fellowship, the church, decides to help us rather than just watch from a distance. I once asked a Reformed Presbyterian pastor in the inner city who also works with prisoners, "What gives a person hope that his life could be different in the future?"

"It takes two things," he replied. "The proclamation of the gospel—that Jesus forgives and changes, making new creatures—*linked with* the evidence of acceptance by a Christian community. The second proves that the first was more than just talk."

He went on to tell about a young man, a graduate of a Christian college in his city, who knew all the proper theology but had become a drug addict nonetheless. "He was hooked on methadone, and all the talking in the world wouldn't set him free. What finally turned him around was when one of our deacons took him into his own home for a year and a half. There he saw the doctrine fleshed out, and he was gradually restored."

Church boards and committees that read 1 Corinthians 5 (the disciplining of the man who committed incest) must go on to 2 Corinthians 2 (Paul's follow-up instruction to "forgive and comfort him, so that he will not be overwhelmed"— v. 7). The Scriptures are clear in their call for spiritual leaders to "bind up the brokenhearted,"[1] to bring back the stray sheep of the flock,[2] to "restore him gently."[3] As they reach out in love, their members will do the same, and healing will result.

One man who was ousted from his profession for an indiscretion took work as a hod carrier simply to put bread on the table. He was suddenly plunged into a drastically different world; instead of going to an office each day, he was hauling loads of concrete block up to the fifth level of a construction site. Gone was the piped-in music in the corridors; now he had to endure blaring radios. Any girl who walked by was subject to rude remarks and whistles. Profanity shot through the air, especially from the foreman, whose primary tactics were whining and intimidation: "For—sake, you—, can't you do anything right? I never worked with such a bunch of—in all my life...."

Near the end of the third week, the new employee felt he could take no more. *I'll work till break time this morning*, he told himself, *and then that's it. I'm going home.* He'd already been the butt of more than one joke when his lack of experience caused him to do something foolish. The stories were retold constantly thereafter. *I just can't handle any more of this.*

Awhile later, he decided to finish out the morning and then leave at lunchtime. Shortly before noon, the foreman came around with paychecks. As he handed the man his envelope, he made his first civil comment to him in three weeks.

"Hey, there's a woman working in the front office who knows you. Says she takes care of your kids sometimes."

"Who?"

He named the woman, who sometimes helped in the nursery of the church where the man and his family worshiped. The foreman then went on with his rounds. When the hod carrier opened his envelope, he found, along with his check, a handwritten note from the payroll clerk: "When one part of the body of Christ suffers, we all suffer with it. Just wanted you to know that I'm praying for you these days."

He stared at the note, astonished at God's timing. He hadn't even known the woman worked for this company. Here at his lowest hour, she had given him the courage to go on, to push another wheelbarrow of mortar up that ramp. God had used a fellow believer to rescue his spirit just in time. He stayed with the job until something more suitable came along.

Whether we have the prayerful support and extended love of a church or not, we can still make it. We must not let the shortcomings of one congregation derail us. Their fears and prejudices may make it hard for us, but they do not make it impossible. Our Father will believe in us no matter what.

And we never know when he will move us from one stage to the next, or suddenly launch us out into a bold new venture all at once. "The God of all grace, who called you to his eternal glory in Christ, after you have suffered a little while, will himself restore you and make you strong, firm and steadfast" (1 Peter 5:10). We never see the full picture on any given day. Like a mountain climber struggling up a ravine, we sometimes feel isolated and surrounded by cliffs. But we must remember the goal. We are on our way to the summit. Most of the time it is not within view, but we are headed there regardless. And we will break into the clear eventually.

Along the way, we sometimes battle the fear of falling. More than one forgiven person has been tormented with the fantasy of "What if I blow it again? What if, after all this pain, I am not strong enough to resist temptation?"

The Enemy, of course, would love to engineer a repeat performance. And one of his first strategies toward that end is to get us worrying about it. The more we entertain notions of a second fall, the more vulnerable we become.

But a curious thing happens sometimes. The Devil overplays his hand just a little. If we are alert, we will realize the source of our fears. Near the end of *Perelandra*, C. S. Lewis tells how Ransom is beset in a cave once again by the Un-man, and then "something else came up out of the hole ... branches of trees ... then a tubular mass which reflected the red glow ... long wiry feelers ... the many eyes of a shell-helmeted head ... a huge, many legged, quivering deformity, standing just behind the Un-man so that the horrible shadows of both danced in enormous and united menace on the wall of rock behind them."[4]

Notice how Ransom deals with this threat:

"They want to frighten me," said something in Ransom's brain, and at the same moment he became convinced both that the Un-man had summoned this great crawler and also that the evil thoughts which had preceded the appearance of the enemy had been poured into his own mind by the enemy's will. The knowledge that his thoughts could be thus managed from without did not awake terror but rage. Ransom found that he had risen, that he was approaching the Un-man, that he was saying things, perhaps foolish things, in English. "Do you think I'm going to stand this?" he yelled. "Get out of my brain. It isn't yours, I tell you! Get out of it." As he shouted he had picked up a big, jagged stone from beside the stream. "Ransom," croaked the Un-man, "wait! We're both trapped ..." but Ransom was already upon it.

"In the name of the Father and of the Son and of the Holy Ghost, here goes—I mean Amen," said Ransom, and hurled the stone as hard as he could into the Un-man's face. The Un-man fell as a pencil falls, the face smashed out of all recognition. Ransom did not give it a glance but turned to face the other horror. But where had the horror gone? The creature was there, a curiously shaped creature no doubt, but all loathing had vanished clean out of his mind.... He saw at once that the creature intended him no harm—had indeed no intentions at all. It had been drawn thither by the Un-man, and now stood still, tentatively moving its antennae. Then, apparently not liking its surroundings, it turned laboriously round and began descending into the hole by which it had come.[5]

Such a powerful image shows us exactly what to do with fears of relapse. We must rise against them in the name of our Lord and refuse to be bullied. In the words of Galatians 5:1, "It is for freedom that Christ has set us free. Stand firm, then, and do not let yourselves be burdened again by a yoke of slavery."

God is not interested in failure. He has no reason to want to abandon us to a twilight zone of stagnation. He is committed to seeing us grow, expand, mature, and become ever more useful and fulfilled. Great numbers of his people—our brothers and sisters in Christ—share that dream as well. We can move ahead with anticipation, even excitement. We can start again.

For Your Reflection

1. Name five good things that have occurred in your life in the recent past, and then spend time thanking God for each one specifically.
2. Meditate on Scriptures that speak about *steadfastness* or *firmness*, such as:
   Daniel 6:26
   1 Corinthians 15:58

2 Corinthians 1:3–7
Colossians 2:5
Hebrews 3:12–14
Hebrews 6:16–20
1 Peter 5:6–11
2 Peter 3:17–18

3. Pinpoint any feelings of bitterness you may be nurturing toward persons who have been cool toward you, said unkind things, or whatever. Ask God to wash these feelings out of you and help you rise above them.

The smell of broiled fish lingered in the air as twenty-nine-year-old Jennifer Stermitz pushed back from her in-laws' oak kitchen table. Most of the dinner talk with Greg, her husband, and his parents on this warm June Sunday had centered on the new life now growing in Jennifer's womb. The due date in February seemed far away, but anticipation was already building.

"Thanks for the meal, Mom," said Greg, stretching up to his six-foot, two-inch height and brushing back his thick dark hair. "We'll be on our way now. Jen and I are going to take the tractor out and mow along the aqueduct for the trail ride next Saturday."

The young couple lived next door to Greg's parents on a ranch outside the town of Visalia in California's Central Valley. During the week, Greg worked as a dentist, but he also still helped his father, a retired rancher, with the family business.

As Jennifer's long legs matched her husband's strides across the yard toward the barn, she gazed at the open fields where mares nursed their foals. To her left was the elegant old hacienda built in 1887 that she and Greg planned to restore someday. In the driveway sat their black Cadillac.... Life these days was so different from her meager childhood, she mused, where she had grown up with seven brothers and sisters packed into a plumber's humble abode. The fervent faith of that home had been laid aside as well, although Jennifer still thought of God sometimes. Just that morning she had read Psalm 46:1, "God is our refuge and strength, a very present help in trouble." The words somehow came back to her as she neared the tractor where her husband sat ready to go.

"Hop on!" shouted Greg over the roar of the engine, bringing Jennifer's mind back to the present. She jumped up beside him to perch on the lip of the left wheel guard, clinging with one hand to the tractor seat. It was a warm day, and both of them were in shorts. Greg put the "bush hog" attachment into gear, and soon they were clearing a six-foot swath through the tall grass along the aqueduct.

When they hit a stretch of ragweed, Greg stopped the rig and asked his wife to run back to the house for some long jeans. Running was one of Jennifer's favorite activities. Even in the early stages of pregnancy, she'd done a number of 10K races. In a few minutes she was back with the jeans. But for the moment she just tied them around her waist.

They continued mowing, bouncing over the hidden ruts, ducking under tree branches. All of a sudden, the right back wheel of the tractor heaved upward, having hit a mound hidden in the undergrowth. The tractor lurched to the left, and Jennifer went flying into the air.

"I hardly had time to think," she recalls. "All I could think was *Jump clear of the tractor!* I tried to do that—but at that instant, the tractor wheel grabbed onto the jeans and pulled me underneath."

The tire came up on top of her right hip as it also pinned her left ankle underneath. Pain shot through her limbs. The engine roared, the bush hog blades kept whirring, and gasoline began dripping down upon her. What if the whole thing exploded in flames?

"I shall never forget the stricken look on Greg's face as I stared up from the ground. He frantically worked the gearshift lever, wondering whether to move forward or back —which way would put me at the least risk? Several seconds went by.

"I couldn't scream; it would have done no good any-way. What was going to happen to me? To my baby?! I just kept looking at him … and the stray thought crossed my mind, *That's where all my trust lies, doesn't it? It's all in that one human being these days. What have I done?* My mother would have been ten sentences deep into an impassioned prayer by now. But me? I hadn't used that connection in a long time."

Greg managed to ease the tractor backward at last, freeing Jennifer so she could roll toward the opposite side of the path. Her legs felt warm with blood. She lay gazing up through the tall tree branches toward the blue summer sky. Her husband came running to pick her up.

By the time they got back to the farmstead, she seemed to stabilize a bit. They waited for medical opinion till the next morning, when a visit to the doctor revealed a broken ankle. The baby, however, seemed fine. The lacerations on Jennifer's hip would heal within a couple of weeks.

The young wife breathed a timid prayer of thanksgiving ... even though deep inside she knew that a weight far more crushing than a tractor was still pressing down upon her. The weight of the marriage choice she had made for all the wrong reasons was suffocating her. Would she really be able to save the day? Would the birth of a baby maybe help Greg lessen his rages and become more gentle? Would they ever go to church for more than just social reasons? Would she ever feel truly loved?

It is probably a good thing that, at that moment, Jennifer Stermitz did not know what further heartache awaited her over the next five years. Only when she had been reduced to rubble—a single mom with three preschoolers and no place to live—would she start to find a God-arranged future of stability and happiness.

Church had been a four-times-a-week occurrence for the Lindstrom family when Jennifer was growing up in Fresno, a city of half a million people. And it wasn't just around the corner; church was thirty-three miles west, across the fields in a small town called Mendota, where her parents had felt called to take their burgeoning family. In fact, when Jennifer was in grade school, her dad had become the lay pastor of the little congregation. Every Wednesday and Saturday night, here came the Lindstrom station wagon full of kids. Early Sunday morning they were back again, with a packed lunch so they could stay all day, returning to Fresno late that night.

"Mendota was, in those days, a kind of town where nobody had much money," Jennifer recalls. "Kids dropped out of school by age fourteen to get married and have babies—not always in that order. Our family tried to help people know the Lord and understand the Bible. I remember wonderful times of feeling the Lord's presence in that little church behind the fire station. Church was our whole life, it seemed."

Jennifer was a willing helper in all that transpired at both church and home; being the second oldest of eight, she did more than her share of diaper changing, dishwashing, and also piano playing on Sundays. Everyone who knew her assumed she was on the straight and narrow for life—and so did she.

But underneath, in the hidden recesses of the soul, critical gaps lurked unnoticed. Somehow Jennifer never made a *personal* commitment to Christ. Faith was more of a family thing that all the Lindstroms did; the church meetings were lively and emotional at times; but the heart of this individual girl was never consciously pledged to the Lord she sang and read about.

From her father, whom she dearly loved, she still felt a certain harshness, left over from his days of growing up in a legalistic home. He would say things like "I'm so ashamed that you kids don't read the Bible more." Jennifer would feel guilty in response.

In her adolescent mind, she viewed her weekends in Mendota and the high-achieving school she attended back in Fresno as opposite sides of a cultural canyon. The sons and daughters of California State University professors in her classrooms were obviously going places in life; the small-town kids, she told herself, were going nowhere. And God was clearly part of Mendota, not Fresno. Yet she loved school and did well in her studies. Her whole family valued education.

By the time she became a teenager, she had already reached her full height of five-foot-eight and, with her trim figure and golden hair, was starting to turn heads on the street. But she didn't date, because her father had drilled into her that only Christian boys were eligible, and the only ones she knew were unmotivated dropouts. Nothing else was said in her home about how to choose a life partner. As for the topic of sex, not a word was uttered.

"I finished high school and managed to get a one-year scholarship to Cal State," says Jennifer. "That way I could still live at home to save money. With all our kids, there was no way my folks could help me financially. I worked three jobs to pay for school—even some modeling along the way."

Her first serious relationship didn't happen until age twenty, when a minor-league baseball player began taking her out. He was divorced, and his tastes in entertainment began pulling Jennifer away from her family's standards. Within six months that friendship fizzled, but so had the spiritual embers from her Christian upbringing. She went on to graduate from Cal State–Fresno with a degree in education in three-and-a-half years.

"I was proud of myself and what I'd accomplished, pretty much all alone. I immediately got a job teaching

English and coaching track at a middle school while beginning my master's degree."

A university staff member's son was her next attraction, lasting four years this time. "Kevin was good-looking and chivalrous, and I felt truly appreciated. But spiritually, we had nothing in common. It took a long time for me to realize this wasn't going to work.

"The years kept passing, and the longer I taught, the more I began to feel extreme voids in my life. I would wake up in the middle of the night to something I can only describe as a hunger. Life seemed to be zooming past, and I was getting left on the curb. God and church were just sort of out there in haze somewhere. I was so sad, so empty.

"My life was full of holes, even though I had a great apartment, drove a red Mustang convertible, and held a good job. But still … I couldn't find men who liked what I liked, who enjoyed intellectual topics, who were on the way up in life.

"That's when I got in touch with Greg Stermitz."

Here was a professional man with energy and initiative. He needed a good-looking wife to take to professional meetings; she needed someone to hold her and relieve her loneliness. On their first date, they went horseback riding on his parents' ranch. Their romance lasted for fifteen months, culminating in a beautiful springtime wedding.

"My insecurities were cavernous," says Jennifer now with hindsight. "I had no courage at all. I just knew I wanted to be a mom and have a 'normal' life—which meant you had to get married, right?

"The morning of my wedding, I remember feeling this terrible uneasiness. I went down into the basement of my apartment and pleaded with God for a sense of peace. Other times, that had worked—but this time it wouldn't come. I finally went back upstairs and got dressed for the ceremony."

After a cruise ship honeymoon, the young couple set up housekeeping. Within a few weeks, Jennifer had seen her first angry outburst from Greg. On Memorial Day, she inadvertently punched the door-lock button on the Cadillac while getting out, which locked the car with the engine still running. Greg was livid. He wouldn't let the subject go for the rest of the entire day.

As time went on, she would nervously watch his attention to other women in social settings. Occasionally he would come home late, with alcohol on his breath. He always had an explanation.

In time, a little boy named Michael was born, and two years later, another boy named Kyle. They moved into the restored hacienda and began filling it with beautiful antiques. After much hard work, it was fit for a magazine photographer.

But that didn't help the times when Greg would head to his office on Sunday afternoons, and the phone line would stay busy for hours. Again, Jennifer could only wonder what was really going on. They did manage to concur that it would be nice to have one more child, though—hopefully a daughter this time, who could be named Angela and thus extend a three-generation tradition in the Stermitz family.

Jennifer did the bookkeeping for the dental business, and sometime near the end of August, when she was still in her first trimester, she came across an $800 charge on a Visa bill that was beyond all credibility. She called the Vancouver hotel to check it out, and discovered the awful line items: two suites, one registered in a woman's name, and among other things, a single room-service charge of $200. What she had long suspected, and feared, could no longer be ignored.

"I stood up, walked into our library and sat down in the recliner, stunned," she remembers. "My eyes traveled across the bookshelves by the fireplace. There were titles on chakras, New Age, acupuncture, yoga. I opened one of the books, and there in Greg's handwriting was this quote: 'The more one gets to know oneself, the more godlike one becomes. —Darwin.'

"I couldn't move. I couldn't pray. I couldn't even cry. How could all of this happen right under my nose, and I'd been too preoccupied with life to see it? What was I going to do now?"

When Greg came home late that afternoon and headed upstairs to change clothes, Jennifer confronted him immediately. She stared across their bedroom and said, "Greg, I have a question. Are you having an affair?"

His head came up from the floor. "No," he replied with a touch of irritation.

"Well, you seem to be gone an awful lot these days, and I just notice changes in your attitude toward me."

"I don't know what you're talking about."

"All right, I'll show you what I mean," Jennifer replied, and headed downstairs to get the Visa bill. She was back in a minute.

"Here—explain this," she said, putting the paper in front of his face as he lay on the bed.

Color began creeping up his neck, and he drew in a breath. Then he answered, "Yeah, well, you just don't make me happy anymore. I love you—but this is just not going to work." He swung up from the bed and went downstairs. The next sound Jennifer heard was his car heading down the driveway.

He didn't return until darkness had fallen, and said nothing. The next day's discussion was no better. This marriage was clearly headed for the ditch, baby or no baby. Affairs with other women of the town soon came to the surface.

"One hot afternoon late that week, while my boys were napping," Jennifer recalls, "I felt like I was going to explode. I gathered my Bible and stepped out the door. I walked into the field behind the barn, where mares and geldings stared at me questioningly. I kept walking toward the fence, and they followed me.

"There I sat down on a rock, clutched the Bible to my chest, and prayed the most important prayer of my life:

"God, I am to the end. I don't have any place else to go, no one else to lean on. I used to think that when your husband had an affair, you just got rid of him. But here I am with a three-year-old, a one-year-old, and a third child on the way. God, what do I do?"

She paused for a moment, then stood up and lifted her face to the sky before continuing:

"God, here I am—emptied out. I surrender it all. I give you not only this circumstance but the rest of my life, no matter what that means. Teach me to lean on you."

The rest of fall and winter was not a pretty sight. Jennifer's husband had enough regard for his reputation in Visalia not to leave his pregnant wife completely, although he moved the majority of his clothes to an apartment above his office. His liaison continued unchecked. Arguments with Jennifer intensified, until at times the police had to be called. Twice Greg was fined for physical assault.

She, meanwhile, began to study the Bible's teaching on divorce and to pray fervently for a reconciliation. She saw at last the issues she had skipped during their courtship six years before. She sought the Lord for direction. Couldn't he somehow put the broken pieces back together?

In this case, God's only response was to bolster her composure a day at a time and prepare her for single parenthood.

"I'd been rejected for an older woman, but still," she says, "I never felt prettier than I did during that pregnancy. I gained only about fourteen pounds. I cherished the experience, not really wanting it to be over, because I knew it would be my last time to give birth."

When the child arrived, it was indeed a girl. Greg attended the delivery, although not in a particularly good mood about the timing; it interrupted college basketball's "March Madness," and UCLA was in the Final Four. About ten days later, soon after mother and child came home from the hospital, he cleaned out the last of his clothes. Divorce papers arrived several weeks later.

She felt intense humiliation—in the grocery store, at Michael's preschool, between the church pews. She longed to buy an ad in the local newspaper announcing that she had indeed been a good wife, mother and daughter-in-law. One night as she was talking to God about all the injustices, he seemed to reply, *You've done all you can do. Move on with your life and don't stay behind trying to prove anything to others. Those who matter already know.*

"I didn't have any plans," says Jennifer. "I had hired an attorney with no more instruction than 'Just protect me, please.' He said I should at least seek financial maintenance so I could go back to school. I followed his lead, but my mind was too consumed with caring for my children to think about much else."

God was indeed thinking about the future, however. Throughout the spring and summer he sustained her emotions and helped her stay afloat financially. One night Jennifer had a dream. She saw herself in a college building, talking across the desk to an older gentlemen who said he had been a dean but was now semi-retired. He still came by to help students from time to time.

Several weeks later, Jennifer decided that if she wanted any chance of furthering her education, she had probably better get busy with research. She set a day, got a baby-sitter, and drove the seventy miles south to Bakersfield, where Cal State had another campus.

Standing in the Education Building lobby as professors and students whizzed by, she looked around wondering what to do next. Whom should she talk to? She had no leads to follow, no prearranged appointments.

Gazing at the directory, she chose a name at random, took the elevator to the third floor, and walked in. An older man sat at a desk. He looked up with an approachable expression on his face.

"Hello? My name is Jennifer Stermitz, and I was wondering about a possible graduate program...."

"Certainly. Let's talk."

Before the day was done, the man—a former dean now advising students—had mapped out a comprehensive three-year route to a doctorate. She floated back to Visalia that day with a huge smile that wouldn't go away. She had thought there was no future—but God had made a way. Within a few weeks the advisor had arranged *a full-ride fellowship to pay the entire tuition plus $7,500 a year in cash* for being a teaching assistant.

The man's wife was a realtor, and she helped find an apartment complex that would accept three children. Nearby was a church that turned out to be a nurturing haven for Jennifer and her kids. Her life was hectic, what with juggling classwork, day-care arrangements, and meeting the emotional needs of her little brood. But her anchor was fixed in a God who had not abandoned her in her desperate hour. He would see her through.

"I didn't know what courage was until I became a single mom," she says. "I had never stood up to difficulty. I'd never made myself be tough and in charge. Now I had little choice but to grab the decisions of my life, find out what God wanted, and then do it."

The divorce became final on December 23. "Sitting in court that day, as the attorneys wrangled back and forth, the thought came to me that the success of my little family's future did not hinge on the provisions of my husband. God had assured me that we would be okay, no matter what."

After her first year of coursework, Jennifer's ingenious realtor friend even managed to help her buy a modest house—quite a trick for an unmarried woman with three dependents living on $7,500 a year plus child support. During that year, she faced the threat that child support would be reduced. The court hearing date hit right in the middle of a flurry of scholastic deadlines, and Jennifer was so swamped she felt she had no time to prepare a defense. "The Lord impressed me with the Scripture in Matthew 10 where Jesus told the disciples, 'They will deliver you up to the courts.... But when they deliver you up, do not become anxious about how or what you will speak; for it shall be given you in that hour what you are to speak. For it is not you who speak, but it is the Spirit of your Father who speaks in you' (Matt. 10:17, 19, 19, NASB).

"We went to court that day, back to the same courtroom where the divorce had been granted—and all of a sudden, my ex-husband withdrew his claim!"

Jennifer's Ph.D. degree, dissertation and all, was finished at last, and the university hired her to teach full-time—despite a standing policy against hiring their own graduates. Jennifer still doesn't know why she got the job. At the end of that year, the rule was belatedly enforced, so that she could not return. She started her own motivational speaking and consulting business, addressing audiences in corporations, schools, and church groups. When the cash flow proved to be irregular, however, her undergraduate alma mater back in Fresno called to ask if she would consider a faculty position there. Time and again, God showed that he was simply not going to let this single-parent family sink beneath the waves.

The biggest provision, however, came the week of her forty-second birthday, when the phone rang one evening. A producer from a Christian television network said they were starting a new weekend program for single parents, and would she like to audition for the job of host?

Today, Dr. Jennifer Lindstrom (she has reverted to her original surname) and her growing children live in the Los Angeles metroplex, where she goes before the cameras each week and tells thousands of viewers just like herself that while God did not ordain their circumstances, he is more than aware of what they are going through and cares deeply about their stresses. He is the still the God of the fatherless, the widow, the misunderstood, the abandoned.

In her journal, Jennifer writes eloquent reflections like the following:

> The afternoon sun spotlights the crimson edges of the leaves in the yard. Hues of golds, burgundies, yellows, browns and deep greens line the horizon as far as the eye can see. A crisp wind filters through the opening of the window where I sit, thinking....
>
> The children burst through the doors from school, dropping their backpacks. They search for something to fill their tummies as they gush about their

day's activities: spelling test results, paint spilled during art, a new friend found at recess....

Little Angela, my "angel," pauses for a hug, then runs to her room.... Kyle pitches his jacket onto the shelf beneath his trophies as he scoops up his guinea pig.... Michael reaches for his rollerblades and knee pads to head for the sidewalk outside.

This is an ordinary day in what the world still sometimes describes as "a broken home." The normalcy of it reflects God's bountiful riches.... I have no desire to return to the life I came from, to the things I held so closely and fought so hard to keep. Instead, I say, in the words of Samuel of old, "Hitherto hath the Lord helped us." If anything, my eyes are fixed rather on the city that lies ahead, the better country, where God himself shall wipe away all regrets.

The serenity of such moments for Jennifer Lindstrom does not mean that life has become tension-free. She and Greg occasionally still have disagreeable phone calls. "But God has been leading me to turn loose of whatever still binds me, to let it all go," she says. "Yes, it's tough with irregular child support—but we're managing. My children are growing tall now and learning to follow God for themselves. I have never loved getting up and going to work so much as I do now. This is home.

"The bad choice of my past is now being leveraged for good. Isn't that just like our God?"

When David Steiner first came as a young seminary graduate to Lake Sparrow Camp,[1] it was not much more than a clearing in the birch and spruce forests of Ontario. The roughhewn lodge that served as both meeting place and dining hall had a leaky roof and uncaulked windows, while the swimming area needed dredging. David and his young bride, Marilee, rented a small apartment in nearby Stanton until a residence could be built on the camp property.

Seven years later, thanks to the hard work of the Steiners and a helpful synod of churches, the camp was busy, well-equipped, and financially healthy. Up to three hundred young people packed its twenty-two cabins each week of the summer, their parents came for fall and spring retreats, and their older brothers and sisters in college gathered at Christmas vacationtime. David, Marilee, and young Randy now lived in a three-bedroom chalet overlooking the lake, and David was often asked to speak to church groups about the innovative trail camping program he had launched.

His fall from the heights was, unfortunately, even swifter than his rise.

Among his enthusiastic staff was Jill Boudreau, an efficient, attractive woman who could teach kids to make almost anything out of leather, ceramic, or wood. She and her husband, a Stanton carpenter, had been among the first to welcome the Steiners to the little town, and when David was ready to hire a handcraft director for the camp staff, she had been a natural choice. Throughout the summers they conferred almost daily about supplies to be ordered, schedules to be adjusted, and the spiritual results they both desired among the campers.

David talks about the time when their contact began to be more than just routine.

"It wasn't a case of my having a bad marriage and therefore reaching out for someone else—not at all. That may have been true with her, but not with me. We were just together a lot, and the trouble was, I began to have feelings for her and didn't put a stop to them.

"There were times when the Holy Spirit would deal with me, even before the relationship became physical. And I would sense conviction; I would pray and ask God to help me. But there was no change in my behavior when I was around her. This happened several times, and then it seemed as if the Holy Spirit sort of stopped bothering me."

Their rendezvous were well planned, so that neither Marilee nor others at the camp suspected. The only trace was David's internal unrest. Around a roaring fire in the evenings, he was still the bright, witty camp director, telling jokes one minute but winding up his talks with questions to make the kids think. More than a few of them responded to his calls for commitment to Christ.

"On the inside, though," he remembers, "it was all I could do to cope with the day-to-day problems of running a camp. It's hard to hear the whispers of other people when you're screaming inside."

Suddenly one day, an inquiry came from an established camp outside Omaha, Nebraska, looking for a director. The thought of moving a thousand miles to an entirely new scene brought relief to his mind; perhaps he could escape the relationship that seemed to be devouring him. The arrangements were discussed with the sponsoring denomination. Marilee was willing to relocate, and as soon as the summer program ended in late August, the Steiners said good-bye to friends and Marilee's parents and headed for the United States.

"I plunged into the work of reorganizing and expanding the program," the husky, dark-haired former halfback says, "but somehow, it wasn't as easy to forget Jill as I thought. The move really didn't solve anything; it just made the phone calls more expensive. In fact, I became so desperate to see her again that I did something rather pitiful: I concocted a trip to a convention in Detroit in November just so she could drive down from Stanton and spend the night."

Her cover-up began to unravel throughout the winter, just as Marilee began to wonder why their monthly phone bill included so many calls back to Ontario. Surely her husband didn't have that many loose ends to tie. The facts finally surfaced in the spring, awkwardly. Marilee's mother came down for a visit and, having been informed by Jill's husband, broke the news to her daughter. Through her tears, Marilee cried, "I couldn't figure out what was the matter. . . . Now it all adds up."

David did not try to deny his mother-in-law's story, but neither was he ready to confess and change. "I withdrew into a lot of hardness and distance from that point on," he says. "I really turned against Marilee emotionally. To paraphrase what Jesus said, no man can love two women. It just won't work. You end up clinging to the one as you despise the other. That's exactly what happened in my case.

"My brother came to see me at one point and said, 'David, do you realize what you're doing to yourself? To your career? There are some occupations where you can get away with this kind of stuff, but yours isn't one of them. As soon as the presbytery finds out, it's all over.'

"To which I replied, 'You know what? I really don't care. I don't feel love for Marilee anymore, and I'm not going to try and fake it. Whatever happens, happens.'"

In order to escape public embarrassment, David submitted his resignation in July, citing "my inability to cope at the present time with various pressures."

The shocked presbytery urged him to take a leave of absence, to try to work out his problem and then come back. He politely declined and began looking for a job, any job, that would give him anonymity. He soon found it, selling institutional kitchen equipment, traveling to call on school districts and hospitals throughout Iowa, Nebraska, and the eastern part of South Dakota.

He would often be gone five days at a time, leaving Monday morning and not returning until Friday or even Saturday as he drove from county seat to county seat across the open plains. "That was just as well—I really didn't want to be home. As long as I could be out there by myself, making a living, I didn't have to face what I was doing to my marriage. I could stop at a phone booth to call Canada whenever I wanted, and no one needed to know.

"But when I'd come home on the weekends, it was strange—I couldn't find a lot of reasons to complain. There was never any great outburst of anger from Marilee, just sadness. She was an incredibly strong woman through it all. About all she would say is 'David, don't you want to talk about things between us? Let's talk.' I'd brush her away with 'Look—I don't want to argue with you'—and go turn on the TV or something.

"I did consider separation for a while. The question in my mind was: *Does Marilee go out the window along with my career?* My principles said no, of course, and the job was providing a separation of sorts as it was. So I didn't do anything drastic; we just moved across the river to Denison, Iowa, in time to get Randy into school that September, and life went on in a kind of dull truce."

There was a tense moment one Sunday when the carpenter called person-to-person to talk to David. His message was desperate: *Please stop making contact with my wife.*

David ventured no promises. What finally did force a halt was when the new director of the Ontario camp called in the late fall. "David," he announced, "a number of people here are now aware of your illicit relationship. All I can say is that if you don't cut it off *now*, I have no choice but to expose you and her before the entire board of directors. That will, of course, result in her having to leave, and it will damage your reputation forever."

David told the man he ought to mind his own business—but when he hung up the phone, he knew he had been outmaneuvered. He would not put his lover through a public exposure. From that day on, he would make no further contact.

But would he recommit himself to Marilee? A test occurred a few weeks later when he announced a nine-day trip through the western part of his territory with his regional manager.

"Will you be back in time for my birthday?" she asked.

David looked again at his calendar. "I don't know," he replied.

Marilee brushed back a strand of her long hair, took a deep breath, and then said softly, "If you're not, I won't be here when you return."

David pondered that for half an hour, then called his manager to say, "I can't go. Can we reschedule the trip?"

David Steiner's intermission lasted more than three years. How much of that was needed and how much was due to his reluctance to make an open confession is hard to say. He fought throughout the first year with self-hatred and bitterness. "If you had asked me who in the Bible I was most like," he says, "I would probably have named Adam. I had gotten myself thrown out of the garden, with absolutely no chance of return, I thought. Now I was banished.

"I didn't go to church: Marilee and Randy went without me. She'd sometimes put my Bible in my suitcase when I'd get ready to leave on a trip, but I'd ignore it. I didn't read the Bible for a long time—I didn't want to be confronted. I was estranged from the Lord, too—not just her.

"The job, in some ways, was good therapy for me. For one thing, it kept me out of the house. For another, it gave me something very concrete to accomplish. There was no ambiguity: I could look back on a trip and say, 'I sold x number of dishwashers, which means x amount of commission; I drove eleven hundred miles: I made each appointment on time; I talked one state trooper out of a speeding ticket,' and so on. I didn't have to debate what to do or whether I'd succeeded or failed; I knew right away."

Sometimes while driving along, his mind would toy with a question: *What might God have to do to get my attention?* Would he touch Randy, for example? The boy seemed not to pay much attention to his parents' problems, but then again, there was a coldness about him those days—was that partly David's fault?

"Marilee told me once, a bit wistfully, that an elderly woman had come up to her in church one day and said, 'You know, dear, I'm just really praying for your husband that he'll be saved.' We kind of had a nervous laugh together about that. But the truth was, the Lord was gradually pulling me back to himself. He was reminding me that I'd made a life commitment to Marilee, and that I'd only be happy as I stayed with that commitment."

The rebuilding of their relationship could be measured only in inches. "The first visible evidence of softening on my part," David remembers, "was when I found myself planning shorter road trips. After a year or so, it seemed as if I didn't want to be gone a week at a time anymore. I began figuring out how to get back to Denison on Wednesday, then go out again. My feelings were catching up with what I'd been doing out of obligation."

David eventually began attending church on Sunday mornings with his family, which put him back into contact with the Scriptures. Psalm 51 gave him the words to express his inner feelings:

> Create in me a pure heart, O God,
>   and renew a steadfast spirit within me.
> Do not cast me from your presence
>   or take your Holy Spirit from me.
> Restore to me the joy of your salvation
>   and grant me a willing spirit, to sustain me.
>
> Psalm 51:10–12

"I came to *want* to be steadfast again, dependable, reliable. And I saw that the first thing to be restored was not my reputation or even my marriage: it was the joy of my salvation, my spiritual relationship with God. If that were right, the rest would follow."

Marilee would occasionally raise the idea of going back to a camp ministry, but David would say, "No, not yet: I'm not ready." Sometime during the second year, the pastor asked if David would be willing to help lead the boys' club on an overnight camp-out. "I sputtered and made excuses, telling him I was sure I'd be out of town that weekend. He simply said to check my calendar, and he'd call me later to see if I could. Before I knew it, I had become part of the club staff— not only to help organize games but to lead devotions, too.

"When a person is in the middle of this kind of process, you really wonder how it will come out in the end. You just have to go a step at a time. Things were gradually improving between Marilee and me; we were talking more, laughing more, enjoying each other more. We finally got to the place where we could talk calmly about the past, and I could tell her how sorry I was for what I'd done. Her forgiving attitude made me wish I'd said those things a lot sooner."

Sometimes the two would fantasize about returning to their former work. What would it be like? They assumed they would probably have to start at the bottom again in a small, run-down camp somewhere. David got up the courage to drop in at a convention of camping administrators for half a day one time, where the reception was generally cordial. One of the men who knew the full story made a point to huddle with him and urge him to think about returning.

The next fall, he took on full responsibility for the boys' club, arranging his schedule to be home for the weekly meetings. The rising happiness in Marilee's face was matched by the words of encouragement that continued to flow from relatives. David's brother loaned him a cassette of a sermon on Romans 8:1—"Therefore, there is now no condemnation for those who are in Christ Jesus." The speaker, Judson Cornwall, concluded with the story of his vision of the diary (told earlier in this book; see pages 105–108). "I listened to that tape mile after mile," David says. "It was a tremendous boost to my spirit."

With the coming of spring, two things happened in close succession to signal a new beginning. First, Marilee discovered that a baby was on the way. She and David were equally excited—"It was like a seal upon our marriage, that we really had weathered the storm and God was now giving us a new life to cherish," she says. "A girl, we hoped!"

The second thing was a phone call from the chairman of a camp board in Colorado Springs. Would David like to consider a position as director of a 270-acre facility in the Rockies?

"I absolutely panicked," David remembers. "My immediate reaction was *No way!*—only I couldn't figure out how to express that politely over the phone. He talked me into agreeing to fly out to look over the camp and discuss the position.

"I can't tell you the agonizing that went on in that blue Chevy the next two weeks as I drove to my various appointments, arguing with myself about whether I was ready. The situation was further complicated by *another* phone call from an even larger retreat ranch in Texas. As it turned out, that was entirely too high-powered for me at this stage; the Colorado responsibility would be all I could handle, if that."

The trip went well enough, the salary was acceptable, the management structure seemed friendly, and David could find no reasonable excuse to turn it down. He and Marilee continued to pray, together as well as individually, for divine guidance. When the formal offer arrived in the mail April 10, they took a big gulp and wrote back an acceptance.

Their house in Denison was sold almost without effort, and the move went smoothly. David began working in mid-May, getting acquainted with camp procedures, meeting personnel, and checking over the plans that had been made for the summer. He discovered right away that two of his four activity directors were women.

"I had to do some fast thinking and praying about how I would relate to them," he says. "My first instinct was to keep my distance, to avoid any contact beyond what was absolutely essential. I've since been able to moderate that to some degree. But I suppose I'm still hesitant when it comes to developing close working relationships with women.

"I've been forced to lean on the Lord's strength, to keep remembering Paul's words about God's power being made perfect in our weakness."

An even greater challenge came his way the second week when a food salesman stopped in to see him. He made his presentation, David placed an order . . . but then the man began to unburden himself about his own personal life. He had committed adultery for the first time within the past two weeks, and he was paralyzed by two fears: What if his wife found out, and what if he had picked up a disease?

"I stood there in the empty pantry almost speechless," David remembers, "trying to listen closely to him, but thinking at the same time, *Why me?! What can I say? I was supposed to take things nice and easy for a while yet . . . why did the Lord put me in this situation?*

"I finally started to explain a few things about the Lord's ability to forgive us, and the longer I talked, the more I could sense the Holy Spirit helping me get the words out. I pulled my New Testament from my pocket and shared some Scripture with him. Tears came to his eyes; we ended up praying together."

Before the man left, David suggested that he see a doctor, to allay his fear of an STD. He also gave the man his "No Condemnation" cassette tape.

"It was good for me to have to try to help someone in a situation similar to mine," David says now. "The Lord steered me through it, and in the end, I was grateful for the challenge. The guy told me later that the tape had meant a great deal."

That first summer went surprisingly well at the camp, in spite of David's late arrival to take the reins. Teenagers from the inner city, from small towns and farms came to swim, eat, climb, compete, laugh, ride horses, and listen to the Word of God. Some of them made life-changing decisions.

And before the Christmas group arrived, a new member had joined the camp staff: six-and-one-half-pound, blue-eyed Stephanie Joy.

The next year saw the birth of a stress camping program like the one David had pioneered in Ontario. The off-season uses of the camp flourished as well.

When David Steiner thinks about past days, he does not ignore the consequences. "The truth is, I can never go back to Stanton," he admits matter-of-factly. "Satan likes to remind me of things like that occasionally, especially when I'm tired or depressed. And there are times when life gets hectic here, and I just want to jump in a car and drive across Nebraska again.

"But the Lord helps me then, too, to get my head back into the present, back to the work he's given me to do here. All things considered, I can hardly believe the Lord could be this good to us."

Marilee's comment in a letter to her sister-in-law perhaps sums it up best: "David is more like the David I married—only things are better now, because we both learned so much through our hard time."

the Restorer

If God is at all involved
with our years
on this planet . . .
if he means to do more
than just watch
from some celestial outpost—
what can we expect?
Will things go from bad to worse . . .
or from bad to better?

He is God.
And whenever he takes the reins,
whenever we give him charge,
things do not deteriorate.
They improve.
They cannot help improving.

Now to him
who is able to do
immeasurably more
than all we ask
or imagine,
according to his power that is at work
within us,
to him be glory . . .
throughout all generations
for ever and ever!
Ephesians 3:20–21

notes

Facing Facts

1. Walter A. Maier, *He Will Abundantly Pardon* (St. Louis: Concordia, 1948), p. 76.

2. Don Osgood, *Pressure Points* (Chappaqua, N.Y.: Christian Herald Books, 1978), p. 13.

What Do I Do with the Memories?

1. Haddon Robinson, "Focal Point" Newsletter (Denver: Conservative Baptist Theological Seminary, 1980).

2. E. M. Blaiklock, *Cities of the New Testament* (Westwood, N.J.: Revell, 1965), pp. 43–44.

A Time to Speak

1. Bruce Narramore and Bill Counts, *Freedom from Guilt* (Irvine, Calif.: Harvest House, 1974), p. 81.

2. Gwynn Lewis, *Nightmare in Paradise* (Old Tappan, N.J.: Spire, 1978), p. 94.

Free Indeed

1. Richard D. Dobbins, "The Psychological Benefits of Sanctification" cassette with notes (Akron: Emerge Ministries, 1979).

2. Narramore and Counts, *Freedom from Guilt*, p. 124.

3. Ibid., p. 131.

New Things

1. Erwin W. Lutzer, *Failure: The Back Door to Success* (Chicago: Moody, 1975), pp. 83–84.

2. Ibid., p. 89.

The Making of a Conqueror

1. Isaiah 61:1–3
2. Ezekiel 34:1–16; also see Zechariah 11:15–17
3. Galatians 6:1–2
4. C. S. Lewis, *Perelandra* (New York: Macmillan, 1944), p. 181.
5. Ibid., pp. 181–82.

Profile: Joy After the Storm

1. Names and other identifications in this profile have been changed at the request of the subjects.

We want to hear from you. Please send your comments about this book to us in care of the address below. Thank you.